First World War
and Army of Occupation
War Diary
France, Belgium and Germany

50 DIVISION
151 Infantry Brigade,
Brigade Machine Gun Company
7 February 1916 - 31 March 1918

WO95/2843/6

The Naval & Military Press Ltd
www.nmarchive.com
Published in association with The National Archives

Published by

The Naval & Military Press Ltd

Unit 10 Ridgewood Industrial Park,

Uckfield, East Sussex,

TN22 5QE England

Tel: +44 (0) 1825 749494

www.naval-military-press.com

www.nmarchive.com

This diary has been reprinted in facsimile from the original. Any imperfections are inevitably reproduced and the quality may fall short of modern type and cartographic standards.

© **Crown Copyright**
Images reproduced by permission of The National Archives, London, England, 2015.

Contents

Document type	Place/Title	Date From	Date To
Heading	WO95/2843/6 151 Inf. Brig. Brigade M/G Co. 1916 Feb-1918 March		
Heading	50th Division 151st Infy Bde 151st Machine Gun Coy. Feb 1916-Mar 1918		
War Diary	Sanctuary Wood	07/02/1916	11/02/1916
War Diary	Dickebusch	12/02/1916	16/02/1916
War Diary	Hill 60	17/02/1916	21/03/1916
War Diary	The Bluff (North Ypres-Comines Canal)	22/03/1916	22/03/1916
War Diary	The Bluff	23/03/1916	31/03/1916
War Diary	The Bluff N of Ypres-Comines Canal	01/04/1916	08/04/1916
War Diary	La Clytte	08/04/1916	21/04/1916
War Diary	Fletre	22/04/1916	25/05/1916
War Diary	La Clytte	26/05/1916	30/06/1916
Heading	151st Machine Gun Company. War Diary. July, 1916. Volume No 6		
War Diary	La Clytte	01/07/1916	16/07/1916
War Diary	Boeschepe	18/07/1916	19/07/1916
War Diary	Kemmel Hill	20/07/1916	31/07/1916
Map	Positions Occupied by 151st Machine Gun Company, East of Kemmel.		
Heading	War Diary 151st Machine Gun Company August 1916 Volume No 3		
War Diary	Kemmel	01/08/1916	10/08/1916
War Diary	Candas	11/08/1916	11/08/1916
War Diary	Ribaucourt	12/08/1916	14/08/1916
War Diary	Vignacourt	15/08/1916	15/08/1916
War Diary	Baizieux	16/08/1916	31/08/1916
Miscellaneous	Supplement to War Diary of 151 Machine Gun Company. Formation of Company.	01/08/1916	01/08/1916
Heading	151st. Infantry Brigade 50th. Division 151st. Machine Gun Company September 1916		
Heading	War Diary of 151 Machine Gun Company From 1st Sept 1916 To 30th Sept. 1916 Volume No 4		
War Diary	Baizieux	01/09/1916	09/09/1916
War Diary	Becourt	10/09/1916	14/09/1916
War Diary	Mametz Wood	15/09/1916	15/09/1916
War Diary	Quarry	16/09/1916	19/09/1916
War Diary	Mametz Wood	20/09/1916	27/09/1916
War Diary	Mametz Wood	26/09/1916	28/09/1916
War Diary	Quarry	28/09/1916	30/09/1916
Heading	War Diary October 1916 151 Machine Gun Coy Volume No 9		
War Diary	Trenches Near Eaucourt L'Abbaye	01/10/1916	04/10/1916
War Diary	Henencourt	05/10/1916	20/10/1916
War Diary	Henencourt	12/10/1916	23/10/1916
War Diary	Becourt	23/10/1916	31/10/1916
Heading	War Diary Of 151 Machine Gun Company For Month Of November 1916 (1st To 30th November 1916) Volume No 6		
War Diary	In the Field	01/11/1916	03/11/1916

War Diary	In Trenches Near Bulte de Warlencourt	03/11/1916	30/11/1916
War Diary	In the Field	02/11/1916	22/11/1916
War Diary	In the Field	03/11/1916	20/11/1916
Heading	War Diary 151st Machine Gun Company 30th November to 31st December Volume No 7		
War Diary	In the Field	01/12/1916	31/12/1916
Heading	War Diary Of 151 Machine Gun Company. From 1st January 1917 To 31st January 1917 Volume 8		
War Diary	In the Field	01/01/1917	31/01/1917
Miscellaneous	Appendix I	09/01/1917	09/01/1917
Map	Map Showing 10 Positions Occupied by 151 MS. Company 20-1-17 Appendix II		
Heading	War Diary Of 151 Machine Gun Coy From 1st Feb 1917 To 28th Feb 1917 Volume 9		
War Diary	In the Field	01/02/1917	28/02/1917
Miscellaneous	151 M/Gun Coy. Training Programme Feb 1st to Feb 8th 1917	01/02/1917	01/02/1917
Heading	151st Machine Gun Company. March 1917. Volume 14		
Heading	War Diary of 151 Machine Gun Company. From 1st to 31st March 1917 Volume XIV		
War Diary	In the Field	01/03/1917	31/03/1917
Miscellaneous	151 M/Gun Coy Training Programme 1st Week Appendix 1 (a)	12/03/1917	12/03/1917
Miscellaneous	151st M. Gun Coy Training Programme 2nd Week Appendix 1 (B)	19/03/1917	19/03/1917
Miscellaneous	151st Machine Gun Coy Training Programme Appendix 1 (C)	24/03/1917	24/03/1917
Heading	War Diary of 151 Machine Gun Company. From 1st to 30th April 1917 Volume No XI		
War Diary	La Vicogne	01/04/1917	01/04/1917
War Diary	Gezaincourt	02/04/1917	02/04/1917
War Diary	Ligny-Sur Canche	03/04/1917	03/04/1917
War Diary	Criselles	04/04/1917	06/04/1917
War Diary	Fouhlin	07/04/1917	07/04/1917
War Diary	Ricametz Ambrines	08/04/1917	09/04/1917
War Diary	Agnez Les Duisans	10/04/1917	10/04/1917
War Diary	Ronville Caves	11/04/1917	11/04/1917
War Diary	Ronville	12/04/1917	22/04/1917
War Diary	Wancourt	22/04/1917	23/04/1917
War Diary	Wancourt Tower Ridge	24/04/1917	25/04/1917
War Diary	Ronville	26/04/1917	26/04/1917
War Diary	Arras	27/04/1917	27/04/1917
War Diary	Humbercourt	27/04/1917	30/04/1917
War Diary	In the Field	03/04/1917	22/04/1917
War Diary	In the Field	18/04/1917	25/04/1917
War Diary	In the Field	14/04/1917	24/04/1917
War Diary	In the Field	07/04/1917	28/04/1917
Heading	War Diary 151st Machine Gun Company. May 1917 Volume 12		
Heading	War Diary 151st Machine Gun Company Volume XVI May 1st To 31st 1917		
War Diary	Humbercourt	01/05/1917	01/05/1917
War Diary	Pommier	02/05/1917	02/05/1917
War Diary	Bailleulval	03/05/1917	04/05/1917
War Diary	Humbercourt	05/05/1917	17/05/1917
War Diary	Monchy au Bois	18/05/1917	23/05/1917

War Diary	Saulty	24/05/1917	24/05/1917
War Diary	Souastre	25/05/1917	31/05/1917
Heading	War Diary. 151st Machine Gun Company June 1917. Volume 17		
Heading	War Diary of 151st Machine Gun Company June 1st-30th 1917 Volume XVII		
War Diary	Souastre	01/06/1917	14/06/1917
War Diary	Nr Mercatel	15/06/1917	16/06/1917
War Diary	Nr Heninel	17/06/1917	29/06/1917
War Diary	Nr Mercatel	30/06/1917	30/06/1917
Miscellaneous	Training Programme		
Miscellaneous	Training Programme Appendix I		
Miscellaneous	Training Programme		
Heading	War Diary 151st Machine Gun Coy July 1917 Volume No XVIII		
Heading	151		
Heading	War Diary 151st Machine Gun Company July 1917 Volume XVIII		
War Diary	Mercatel	01/07/1917	02/07/1917
War Diary	N.16.d.1.7	03/07/1917	18/07/1917
War Diary	Mercatel	19/07/1917	29/07/1917
War Diary	N 22 d 9.2	30/07/1917	31/07/1917
Heading	War Diary. 151st Machine Gun Company. August 1917. Volume XIX		
War Diary	Heninel	01/08/1917	12/08/1917
War Diary	Near Mercatel	13/08/1917	19/08/1917
War Diary	Wancourt Feuchy Line	20/08/1917	31/08/1917
Miscellaneous	151st M.G. Coy Training Programme.	13/08/1917	13/08/1917
Heading	War Diary 151st Machine Gun Company September 1917 Volume XX		
War Diary	Cojuel Valley Sector	01/09/1917	02/09/1917
War Diary	N.16.B.18. Coy. H.Q.	02/09/1917	03/09/1917
War Diary	Carlisle Lines Beaurains.	04/09/1917	04/09/1917
War Diary	M.16.d.9.1	05/09/1917	12/09/1917
War Diary	Cherisy Sector	13/09/1917	13/09/1917
War Diary	Coy H.Q. at M.16.B.9.1.	14/09/1917	21/09/1917
War Diary	Cherisy Sector	22/09/1917	29/09/1917
War Diary	Carlisle Lines.	30/09/1917	30/09/1917
War Diary	Nr Beaurains	30/09/1917	30/09/1917
War Diary	M.16.d.9.1	30/09/1917	30/09/1917
Miscellaneous	Report on the Part Taken by the 151st M.G. Coy in Operation of the 15/16, September, 1917, in Front of Cherisy.		
Miscellaneous	Rounds fired and Stop Pages.		
Heading	War Diary 151st Machine Gun Company October 1917. Volume XXI		
War Diary	Carlisle Lines.	01/10/1917	01/10/1917
War Diary	Near Beaurains.	02/10/1917	04/10/1917
War Diary	Gomiecourt	05/10/1917	15/10/1917
War Diary	Gomiecourt and Bapaume	16/10/1917	16/10/1917
War Diary	Near Zeeger's Cappelle	17/10/1917	19/10/1917
War Diary	Ledringham	20/10/1917	20/10/1917
War Diary	Near Proven	21/10/1917	22/10/1917
War Diary	Salem Camp	23/10/1917	25/10/1917
War Diary	Dublin Camp	26/10/1917	28/10/1917
War Diary	Dublin Camp. (A.10.d.6.8)	28/10/1917	31/10/1917

Heading	War Diary 151st Machine Gun Company November, 1917 Volume XXII		
War Diary	U 18 C 5.6 (Sheet 20)	01/11/1917	06/11/1917
War Diary	Dublin Camp	07/11/1917	09/11/1917
War Diary	Moulle	10/11/1917	30/11/1917
War Diary	Moulle	14/11/1917	29/11/1917
Miscellaneous	Training Programme 151st Machine Gun Company From 15th November 1917 To 24th November 1917	12/11/1917	12/11/1917
Miscellaneous	151st Machine Gun Coy Programme Of Training From 25th November 1917 To 30th November 1917	22/11/1917	22/11/1917
War Diary	War Diary of 151st Machine Gun Coy. From Decr 1st 1917 to Decr 31st 1917 Vol 19		
War Diary	Moulle	01/12/1917	08/12/1917
War Diary	Moulle	02/12/1917	10/12/1917
War Diary	Brandhoek	10/12/1917	10/12/1917
War Diary	Potijze & In The Line	11/12/1917	15/12/1917
War Diary	Potijze & In The Line	13/12/1917	19/12/1917
War Diary	Potijze & In The Line	17/12/1917	23/12/1917
War Diary	Potijze & In The Line	20/12/1917	31/12/1917
War Diary	Potijze & In The Line	28/12/1917	29/12/1917
Miscellaneous	151st Machine Gun Company Programme Of Training From 1st December 1917 To 8th December 1917 (both mil)	01/12/1917	01/12/1917
Heading	War Diary Of The 151st Machine Gun Company From 1st To 31st January 1918 Volume XXIV		
War Diary	In The Line & Potijze	01/01/1918	04/01/1918
War Diary	Eecke	05/01/1918	15/01/1918
War Diary	Eecke	11/01/1918	17/01/1918
War Diary	Le Val. D'Acquin	18/01/1918	26/01/1918
War Diary	Le Val. D'Acquin	18/01/1918	25/01/1918
War Diary	Potijze & In The Line	27/01/1918	31/01/1918
Miscellaneous	151st. Machine Gun Company Programme Of Training For Period January 7th To 12th 1918 (both incl.)	07/01/1918	07/01/1918
Miscellaneous	151st Machine Gun Company. Programme Of Training for Period January 13th to 19th 1918	11/01/1918	11/01/1918
Miscellaneous	Programme Of Training For The 151st Machine Gun Company. For Period Jan 20th To 26th 1918	18/01/1918	18/01/1918
Heading	War Diary of 151st Machine Gun Coy From Feby 1st 1918 to Feby 28th 1918		
War Diary	In The Line & Potijze	01/02/1918	04/02/1918
War Diary	In The Line & Potijze	01/02/1918	16/02/1918
War Diary	Potijze	15/02/1918	20/02/1918
War Diary	Le Val D'Acquin	20/02/1918	24/02/1918
War Diary	Le Val D'Acquin	22/02/1918	26/02/1918
War Diary	Le Val D'Acquin	25/02/1918	28/02/1918
Miscellaneous	Programme Of Training For 151st Machine Gun Company From 25th February, 1918 To 28th February 1918 (both mil)	24/02/1918	24/02/1918
Heading	50th Divisional Troops Became "C" Company 50th Machine Gun Battalion 151st Machine Gun Company March 1918		
Heading	C Coy		
War Diary	Le Val D'Acquin	01/03/1918	08/03/1918
War Diary	Glisy	09/03/1918	10/03/1918
War Diary	Harbonnieres	11/03/1918	21/03/1918
War Diary	Harbonnieres	13/03/1918	31/03/1918

War Diary		22/03/1918	31/03/1918
Miscellaneous	151st Machine Gun Company Training Programme, From 3/3/1918 To 7/3/1918 (both mil)	02/03/1918	02/03/1918
Miscellaneous	151st Machine Gun Company Training Programme From 14/3/1918 To 21/3/1918 (both mil)	12/03/1918	12/03/1918

WO 95 2843/6

151 INF. BRIG.

— BRIGADE M/G CO.

1916 FEB — 1918 MARCH

50TH DIVISION
151ST INFY BDE

151ST MACHINE GUN COY.

FEB 1916-MAR 1918

Army Form C. 2118.

WAR DIARY
or
INTELLIGENCE SUMMARY.
(Erase heading not required.)

151 Bde Machine Gun Company
Volume 1
Feb. 1916
p2

NC/A

Place	Date	Hour	Summary of Events and Information	Remarks and references to Appendices
SANCTUARY WOOD	7th		MONDAY PROMENADE DUG-OUTS heavily shelled. Four casualties:- 2024 Pte Armstrong R and 1427 Pte Thompson E killed. 2473 Pte Wade and 1836 Pte Kinton, wounded.	
	8th		TUESDAY SANCTUARY WOOD shelled heavily. GOUROCK ROAD badly damaged.	
	9th		WEDNESDAY Enemy reported to be massing for an attack on the YPRES SALIENT	
	10th		THURSDAY Situation normal.	
	11th		FRIDAY Situation quiet. 151st Inf. Bde. relieved by 149th Inf. Bde.	
DICKEBUSCH	12th		SATURDAY The Machine Gun Company paraded en masse for the first time, opportunities thus occurring for organization considerably lessened by adverse weather conditions.	
	13th		SUNDAY Enemy's attitude to Corps frontage very threatening.	
	14th		MONDAY Enemy attacked and captured the BLUFF from 17th Division. All counter-attacks failed. Brigade ordered to "stand by".	
	15th		TUESDAY Renewed counter attacks by 17th Division failed.	

WAR DIARY or INTELLIGENCE SUMMARY

151 Bde Machine Gun Company

Vol. 1 Feb. 1916 p 3

Place	Date	Hour	Summary of Events and Information	Remarks and references to Appendices
DICKEBUSCH	16th		151 Inf. Bde. reported to be about to be called upon for a counter-attack. Eventually part of the 3rd Division was recalled from G.H.Q reserve.	
	17th		WEDNESDAY. Officers went to look round Hill 60 Sector with a view to taking over. Trenches in very bad condition owing to attacks and counter-attacks at the BLUFF. Enemy sniping deadly.	
HILL 60	17th		THURSDAY 151st Bde. M.G. Coy. relieved 150th Bde. M.G. Coy. on HILL 60. Sections occupied following positions:- A section - A3, Machine gun hanagones, Machine Gun House. B " - 41S, 39S, 2 Dump positions C " - R7, R8, Blauwepoort Farm D " - 4 Maçon X, X Trench, Battersea Farm. 3 guns were in Brigade Reserve at Bedford House.	
	18th		FRIDAY Relief of 150th Inf. Bde. by 151st Inf. Bde. completed. Enemy snipers deadly.	
	19th		SATURDAY had for extra caution results in several men in battalion being sniped. The Brigade for the first time had to submit to	

WAR DIARY
or
INTELLIGENCE SUMMARY.

Army Form C. 2118.

151st Bde Machine Gun Company

Vol 1 p 4
Feb 1916

Place	Date	Hour	Summary of Events and Information	Remarks and references to Appendices
HILL 60	20th		enemy's superiority in sniping, rifle-grenades and trench-mortars	
			SUNDAY Eleven days systematic bombardment of enemy's trenches commenced on the BLUFF.	
	21st		MONDAY Weather bitterly cold. Snow fell during the night.	
	22nd		TUESDAY Situation normal.	
	23rd		WEDNESDAY 3 minnenwerfers fell on DUMP (East side) fired apparently at maximum range.	
	24th		THURSDAY Situation normal.	
	25th		FRIDAY At noon enemy heavily shelled front line. 9th Durham L.I. having many casualties. Weather cold and wet.	
	26th		SATURDAY Enemy made a bomb attack on Brigade on the right, at the same time he heavily shelled trenches in 151st Brigade sector. 9th D.L.I. again suffered heavily. 39S trenched on both sides of M.G. emplacement by 5.9 shells.	
	27th		SUNDAY 41S and Lovers Lane bombed by trench-mortars	
	28th		MONDAY 151 Bde M.G. Coy relieved by 149 M.G. Coy. Our telephone message	

WAR DIARY or INTELLIGENCE SUMMARY

151st Bde Machine Gun Company

Army Form C. 2118.

Vol 1. Feb. 1916

p 5

Place	Date	Hour	Summary of Events and Information	Remarks and references to Appendices
HILL 60			relating to completion of relief apparently overheard by enemy. Each section was shelled on its way to KRUISTRAAT, especially at ZILLEBEK STATION, SHRAPNELL CORNER, TRANSPORT FARM. Fortunately there were no casualties except 2 from shell-shock	
	29th TUESDAY		Relief of 151 Inf. Battalions postponed. Massing for the re-taking of the BLUFF commenced. C & D sections moved to PROMENADE and RAILWAY dug-outs respectively, C section being at the disposal of the G.O.C. 150th Bde. D section at the disposal of the G.O.C. 149th Bde. Situation quiet. Weather rainy	

Vol. 2
March 1916
p.1

WAR DIARY 151st Bde Machine Gun Company.

Army Form C. 2118.

INTELLIGENCE SUMMARY.

Place	Date	Hour	Summary of Events and Information	Remarks and references to Appendices
HILL 60	1st		WEDNESDAY Two hours bombardment before dusk on enemy's trenches from the BLUFF to SANCTUARY WOOD. 151st Inf. Bde. made a feint attack on Hill 60. Casualties few.	
	2nd		THURSDAY Attack before dawn by 3rd Division on the BLUFF. All trenches which had been lost on Feb. 14th were retaken with part of the BEAN in addition. Enemy taken by surprise. In the bombardment which followed 151st Inf. Bde. suffered heavily, the enemy expecting an attack on Hill 60. The Germans counter-attacked on the BLUFF at noon but were repulsed. The CUTTING was heavily shelled throughout the night. No wounded could be brought down from advanced dressing station during the night. All dug-outs in the Cutting were destroyed.	
	3rd		FRIDAY Situation normal. 151st Inf. Bde. relieved by 149 Inf. Bde. Wounded brought down from advanced dressing station to Railway dug-outs.	
	4th		SATURDAY Situation normal. 149 Inf. Bde. repaired damaged	

WAR DIARY 151st Bde Machine Gun Company Army Form C. 2118.
or INTELLIGENCE SUMMARY.

Vol 2. 9/b
March 1917 p2

Place	Date	Hour	Summary of Events and Information	Remarks and references to Appendices
HILL 60	5th		trenches with vigour. Enemy apparently similarly engaged.	
			SUNDAY Enemy C and D sections relieved by A and B sections.	
	6th		MONDAY Situation normal.	
	7th		TUESDAY Enemy snipers very active otherwise situation unchanged	
	8th		WEDNESDAY Lieut Wood 5th Bn. Border Regiment, attd. to the Machine Gun Company transferred to the Royal Flying Corps. Colonel Stuart, G.S.O.1 50th Division with Capt. W.A. Gregson and Capt. Wilkinson sighted new machine gun positions to cover support trenches 38 to 41, information from prisoners captured on march 2nd indicating that the enemy's saps beneath these trenches were nearing completion. British aeroplane brought down near Railway Dug outs.	
	9th		THURSDAY Open machine gun positions made on the DUMP, LARCH WOOD, VERBRANDENMOLEN.	
	10th		FRIDAY C & D sections relieved A & B in Brigade Reserve at PROMENADE DUG-OUTS and RAILWAY DUGOUTS respectively. The emergency positions constructed the previous night were occupied.	

WAR DIARY
or
INTELLIGENCE SUMMARY

Army Form C. 2118.

151st Bde Machine Gun Company.
Vol. 2
March 1916
P3/

Place	Date	Hour	Summary of Events and Information	Remarks and references to Appendices
HILL 60	11th		The RAILWAY CUTTING was heavily shelled during the night. The following are highly commended for bravery during that time:- 1725 Pte. Clarke who with 3 others remained with his gun on LARCH WOOD under heavy shell fire. 2255 Pte. Corouthers who took charge of two parties taking ammunition and rations up the Cutting on separate journeys. 1670 Pte. Benson J. who accompanied him on each occasion 1457 Pte Henshaw and 1920 Pte. Allen who voluntarily took rations to the detachment on LARCH WOOD.	
	11th		SATURDAY machine gun position in KNOWLE FARM occupied covering 40 S 41 S.	
	12th		SUNDAY Weather fine and warmer.	
	13th		MONDAY C and D sections relieved by half company of 151 Bde. M.G. Coy. 151st Bde. M.G.Coy. relieved 149 Bde. M.G. Coy. Sections occupying same groups as on Feb. 14th.	
	14th		TUESDAY 151 Inf. Bde. relieved 149 Inf. Bde. Situation normal.	
	15th		WEDNESDAY Enemy snipers deadly, especially on 47 trench.	

WAR DIARY
or
INTELLIGENCE SUMMARY

Army Form C. 2118.

151st Bde Machine Gun Company.

Vol. 2 March 1916 p4

(Erase heading not required.)

Place	Date	Hour	Summary of Events and Information	Remarks and references to Appendices
HILL 60	16th		THURSDAY Situation normal. Enemy trench-mortared LOVER'S LANE and the front side of the DUMP. Covered way across RAILWAY CUTTING from the DUMP to LOVER'S WALK completed.	
	17th		FRIDAY Situation in trenches normal. Enemy shelled with lacrimatory shells many 18-pounder batteries in the Salient.	
	18th		SATURDAY BLEAUWPOORT FARM shelled; no direct hits. Right. Bn. Headquarters on the DUMP shelled for first time, this was done by a 5.9" Howitzer Battery from HOOGE. 151st Bde M.G. Coy. relieved by 150th Bde M.G. Coy.	
	19th		SUNDAY Rest.	
	20th		MONDAY Section officers visited positions in BLUFF trenches.	
	21st		TUESDAY Rest.	
THE BLUFF [NORTH YPRES-COMINES CANAL]	22nd		WEDNESDAY 151st Bde M.G. Coy. relieved 76th Bde. M.G. Coy. in the BLUFF trenches. The night was very wet and guides uncertain of their gun positions. The sections were grouped as follows :- A section occupied the Tunnel Positions, Pear Tree Walk and Canal Post. B section occupied 4 positions in Gordon Post. C section occupied trenches 35, 36, 37s & Grand Hut Street.	

Army Form C. 2118.

WAR DIARY
or
INTELLIGENCE SUMMARY. 161st Bde. Machine Gun Company.

Vol 2
March 19th
p.5

(Erase heading not required.)

Instructions regarding War Diaries and Intelligence Summaries are contained in F. S. Regs., Part II. and the Staff Manual respectively. Title pages will be prepared in manuscript.

Place	Date	Hour	Summary of Events and Information	Remarks and references to Appendices
THE BLUFF	23rd		D section occupied R10, 2 Bleuxspoort Hedge positions, Sand bag road.	
	24th		THURSDAY Relief of 76th Inf. Bde. by 151 Inf. Bde. completed.	
			FRIDAY Situation normal. Excellent dug-outs and many interesting souvenirs found in the trenches left by the enemy on March 2nd.	
	25th		SATURDAY Front line and supports in very bad condition. Our infantry and apparently enemy also were occupied with repairs and drainage. Result – situation quiet.	
	26th		SUNDAY C.S.M. Halpins salvaged a Vickers machine gun discovered half-buried in the BLUFF.	
	27th		MONDAY 4:30 a.m. 3rd Division exploded a series of mines of record depth and charge in front of ST ELOI and occupied the craters. From 4:30 till 4:40 a.m. enemy barraged on our sector, for the rest of the day situation was normal.	
	28th		TUESDAY Situation unchanged except that enemy made use of sniping opportunities in the LOOP.	
	29th		WEDNESDAY Enemy counter attacks on ST ELOI before dawn repulsed.	

Army Form C. 2118.

WAR DIARY
or
INTELLIGENCE SUMMARY. 151st Bde. Machine Gun Company.

Vol 2. 1916 March p76

(Erase heading not required.)

Place	Date	Hour	Summary of Events and Information	Remarks and references to Appendices
THE BLUFF	30th		THURSDAY Weather improved, there was considerable aeroplane activity, the enemy appearing to have the superiority in the Salient. Enemy had three observation balloons and appeared to be regaining.	
	31st		FRIDAY Situation normal.	

H Morrison
Capt.
Bde M/Gun Company
151 Bde M/Gun Company

WAR DIARY

151st Brigade Machine Gun Company.

INTELLIGENCE SUMMARY

Place	Date	Hour	Summary of Events and Information	Remarks and references to Appendices
The BLUFF	1st		SATURDAY Kingsway dug-outs condemned after a concentrated bombardment from the enemy.	
N. of YPRES—COMINES CANAL	2nd		SUNDAY Gordon Terrace dug-outs heavily shelled, also Chester Farm.	
	3rd		MONDAY Machine Gun Company relieved by 1st Canadian Brigade. Brigade Headquarters dug-outs destroyed by enemy's bombardment during counter-attack on the St Eloi craters. Captain Harter, Brigade major, mortally wounded. 2 Lieut. P.H.Jenwick joined the machine Gun Company.	
	4th		TUESDAY Rest at DICKEBUSCH HUTS. Remainder of units in the Brigade billeted in POPERINGHE.	
	5th		WEDNESDAY Rest.	
	6th		THURSDAY Ditto.	
	7th		FRIDAY Preparations in progress for moving to new sector.	
	8th		SATURDAY Company moved from DICKEBUSCH HUTS to LA CLYTTE marching past the Brigadier-General at N.2.a.2.1. new head-quarters at N.8.c.5¼.8. SCHOOL FARM. Relieved 2nd 15th Bde Machine Gun Company in 4th Canadian	

WAR DIARY or INTELLIGENCE SUMMARY.

151st Brigade Machine Gun Company

Army Form C. 2118.

April 1916 Vol 3 p 2

Place	Date	Hour	Summary of Events and Information	Remarks and references to Appendices
LA CLYTTE			Trenches M1 to O4 inclusive. C section occupied positions in M1, N5, O2, O4. D section occupied EASTERN REDOUBT, WESTERN REDOUBT, CARRÉ FARM. B section occupied CAPTAIN'S POST, MAJORS COPSE, FORT MORROW, FORT TORONTO, and VIERSTRAAT POST. 2 Lieut. Reade joined the Machine Gun Company.	
	9th		Situation normal.	
	10th		MONDAY Counter attack by Canadian Brigade on our left for the St ELOI CRATERS. Attack partially successful.	
	11th		TUESDAY front line heavily shelled, especially M+N trenches.	
	12th		WEDNESDAY Captain W.A. Grierson went to on leave. During his absence Company commanded by Lieut A.M. Gelsthorpe. Inter-section relief. Enemy distinctly more active.	
	13th		THURSDAY Army Commander visited Brigade Headquarters. A M.G emplacement to cover HOLLANDACHASHUR SALIENT to be hurriedly constructed. Meanwhile M.G from FORT MORROW mounted in open position in M2. FORT MORROW evacuated.	

WAR DIARY or INTELLIGENCE SUMMARY.

151st Brigade Machine Gun Company.
April Vol 2
p 3

Army Form C. 2118.

(Erase heading not required.)

Place	Date	Hour	Summary of Events and Information	Remarks and references to Appendices
LA CLYTE	14th		FRIDAY M & N trenches heavily shelled. 5.9" shells narrowly missed emplacement in M1. Strong dug-out completed in CAPTAIN'S POST.	
	15th		SATURDAY Enemy's artillery less active. Heavy bombardment for an hour by "heavies" on HOLLANDACHASHUR SALIENT. Enemy retaliated on to our unoccupied support trenches.	
	16th		SUNDAY M.G. emplacement in N1 completed. Inter-section relief. Lieut Marley thrown off his horse, resulting in a broken leg.	
	17th		MONDAY Enemy artillery less active. The repair of M trenches completed during night by 7th Durham L.I. pioneer battalion. Captain W.A. Grierson returned from leave.	
	18th		TUESDAY Situation normal.	
	19th		WEDNESDAY Situation normal. Officers of relieving brigade taken round the trenches.	
	20th		THURSDAY Situation normal. 2 Lieut Rankin took over command of D section.	
	21st		GOOD FRIDAY Machine Gun Company relieved by 8th Brigade Machine Gun Company.	

WAR DIARY
or
INTELLIGENCE SUMMARY.

151st Brigade Machine Gun Company
vol 3
April
p. 4

Army Form C. 2118.

Place	Date	Hour	Summary of Events and Information	Remarks and references to Appendices
LA CLYTTE			One section with transport left for rest area at 1 p.m. Weather stormy. Relief carried out during heavy shelling.	
FLÊTRE	22d			
	23d		SATURDAY Remainder of Company arrived in rest area 6 a.m.	
	24th		SUNDAY The remainder of brigade arrived in rest area	
	25th		MONDAY Rest	
	26th		TUESDAY Rest	
	27th		WEDNESDAY Rest.	
	28th		THURSDAY Training commenced. Section drill under section officers.	
			FRIDAY Inspection of 151st Inf. Brigade by General Sir Douglas Haig G.C.B., K.C.I.E., K.C.V.O., A.D.C., Commander-in-chief of British Army in the field	
	29th		SATURDAY Training continued. Section and company drill.	
	30th		SUNDAY Brigade ordered to "stand by" at 2 a.m. Gas attack at several points on 5th Corps front. Raid attempted on M & N trenches in front of WYTSCHAETE but held up by machine gun in M1.	

WAR DIARY 151 BRIGADE MACHINE GUN Army Form C. 2118.
or
INTELLIGENCE SUMMARY.
May 1916
Volume 4

Place	Date	Hour	Summary of Events and Information	Remarks and references to Appendices
FLÊTRE	1st		MONDAY Section Drill	
	2nd		TUESDAY Company Drill.	
	3rd		WEDNESDAY Elementary Machine Gun training began.	
	4th		THURSDAY Ditto.	
	5th		FRIDAY Ditto.	
			Inter-Section football matches commenced.	
	6th		SATURDAY Elementary training continued. Football match against 5th Border Regiment: result, lost 4-2.	
	7th		SUNDAY 2 Lieut. McLeod arrived as a reinforcement officer.	
	8th		MONDAY Elementary Machine Gun training continued.	
	9th		TUESDAY Advanced machine gun training. Football match versus 9th Bn. Durham L.I. lost 2-1.	
	10th		WEDNESDAY Advanced training continued.	
	11th		THURSDAY Ditto.	
	12th		FRIDAY Ditto. Football match versus 8th Bn. Durham L.I. Drawn 2-2. Weather very unsettled	

WAR DIARY or INTELLIGENCE SUMMARY.

151st BRIGADE MACHINE GUN COMPANY Army Form C. 2118.

May 1916 Volume 4

p 2.

Place	Date	Hour	Summary of Events and Information	Remarks and references to Appendices
FLÊTRE	13th		SATURDAY 3 officers and 27 men inoculated.	
	14th		SUNDAY Church Parade in conjunction with 6th Bn. Durham L.I.	
	15th		MONDAY Advanced Machine Gun training commenced.	
	16th		TUESDAY Lecture by Brigade Major to officers on tactical use of machine guns. Brigade Cross-Country run resulted in a win for Machine Gun Company (+ Brigade Signallers) which gained the following places. 1st, 3rd, 5th, 6th, 8th.	
	16th		TUESDAY Farewell speech to the Brigade by Brigadier-General Shea C.M.G. D.S.O. on leaving the Brigade to command a Division.	
	17th		WEDNESDAY Brigadier-General P.T. Westmoreland C.M.G. D.S.O. took over command of the Brigade. Brigade sports. Machine Gun Company gained 1st & 3rd places in Mule Race and 2nd place in Officers 120 yards.	
	18th		THURSDAY Training continued.	
	19th		FRIDAY Instruction ended of 16 men from each battalion of the brigade as machine gunners.	

WAR DIARY 151 BRIGADE MACHINE GUN COMPANY

INTELLIGENCE SUMMARY

May 1916
Volume 4
p 3

Army Form C. 2118.

Place	Date	Hour	Summary of Events and Information	Remarks and references to Appendices
FLÊTRE	20th		SATURDAY Training continued. Brigade boxing competition. Representative from Machine Gun Company defeated in final for light-weights. Football match versus 6th Bn. Durham L.I. Won 5-3.	
	21st		SUNDAY Church Parade at 8th Bn. Durham L.I. Headquarters.	
	22nd		MONDAY Limber drill. Tactical training.	
	23rd		TUESDAY Inspection of 50th DIVISION by ARMY COMMANDER, General Sir Herbert Plumer G.C.M.G., K.C.B. Distribution of D.C.M.s and Military Medals. Football match versus 9th Durham L.I. Drawn 2-2.	
	24th		WEDNESDAY Tactical scheme - rearguard action.	
	25th		THURSDAY Lecture to Company by Captain W.A. Grierson.	
LA CLYTTE	26th		FRIDAY Machine Gun Company moved to LA CLYTTE from G.H.Q reserve, relieving 8th BRIGADE MACHINE GUN COMPANY, and reoccupying trenches M1 to O4 inclusive. Company Headquarters in SCHOOL FARM. A section took over positions O4, O2, N1, M1. B section N5, Eastern Redoubt, Western Redoubt, Curé Farm. C section Captain's Post, Mayor's Corner, Fort Hurrah, Fort Toronto, Vierstraat.	

WAR DIARY or INTELLIGENCE SUMMARY

151 Brigade Machine Gun Company

May 1916

Army Form C. 2118.

Place	Date	Hour	Summary of Events and Information	Remarks and references to Appendices
LA CLYTTE	27th		D section with 3 guns in reserve.	
	28th		SATURDAY Situation quiet. Trench mortar bombs constantly troubling front line, but no shells. Our retaliation weak.	
	29th		SUNDAY Situation normal. Work started on strong dug-outs for gun detachments in front line.	
	30th		MONDAY BOIS CARRÉ shelled for 30 minutes.	
	31st		TUESDAY Situation normal. Guns in SUBSIDIARY LINE FIRE NIGHTLY on enemy's Communication trenches, strong points, and rear positions. WEDNESDAY Dug-out in M1 completed, overhead cover consisting of 2 rows iron girders, 4'6" earth. Situation normal.	

Winogrot Capt.
O.C. M.G. Coy.
151st Bde M.G. Company

WAR DIARY
151st BRIGADE MACHINE GUN COMPANY
Army Form C. 2118.

INTELLIGENCE SUMMARY
Volume 5 June 1916
P¹

Place	Date	Hour	Summary of Events and Information	Remarks and references to Appendices
LACLYTTE	JUNE 1st		THURSDAY Situation normal. FORT MORROW position evacuated, thus allowing a complete section to be held in reserve at SCHOOL FARM.	
	2nd		FRIDAY Situation quiet. Naval action off JUTLAND.	
	3rd		SATURDAY Inter-section relief. No warning having been received concerning road from division on right, B section were relieved in front but by C section while trenches were heavily shelled. Three O.R. were wounded:— 4477 Cpl. Holladay N. 8966 Pte. Patten J. 9378 Pte. Walbank.	
	4th		SUNDAY Situation normal.	
	5th		MONDAY Situation normal. Earl Kitchener drowned in H.M.S. "HAMPSHIRE".	
	6th		TUESDAY Enemy more active with trench-mortars. Our retaliation weak.	
	7th		WEDNESDAY Situation quiet. Inter-section relief.	
	8th		THURSDAY Numerous trench mortar bombs dropped near O₁ emplacement. Machine gun emplacement in Canal Farm permanently occupied.	
	9th		FRIDAY Situation normal. Very strong dug-out completed for O₂ emplacement.	
	10th		SATURDAY Enemy more active than usual.	
	11th		SUNDAY Situation quiet. Gun moved from EASTERN REDOUBT, a position constantly shelled, to BEGGERS REST. Intersection relief.	

WAR DIARY

151st BRIGADE MACHINE GUN COMPANY

Volume 5, June 1916

p.2.

Place	Date	Hour	Summary of Events and Information	Remarks and references to Appendices
LA CLYTTE	JUNE 12th		MONDAY Enemy more active than usual with trench mortars.	
	13th		TUESDAY Situation normal. 2 Lieut Jones to hospital. 2 Lieut Jones resumed command of B section.	
	14th		WEDNESDAY Increased activity on both sides. Battalion snipers claim many hits. 1590 Cpl. Hull (attached from 6th D.L.I.) killed by rum-jar in N1.	
	15th		THURSDAY Enemy's machine guns active during hours of darkness. A considerable amount of work commenced on Brigade supports. Enemy's machine gun fire very troublesome to working parties, but the 18-pounders seemed unable to reduce this activity.	
	16th		FRIDAY Gas attack on right of divisional front. Saves guns in the gassed area strenuously effected by the gas.	
	17th		SATURDAY Situation normal. Strong dug-out completed for detachment in N1. All light draft horses exchanged for mules from R.F.A. A draft of 5 well trained men arrived from the Machine Gun Corps.	
	18th		SUNDAY Quiet. Inter-section relief. Company divided into the following	

WAR DIARY
or
INTELLIGENCE SUMMARY.

Army Form C. 2118.

151st BRIGADE MACHINE GUN COMPANY.

Volume 5
June 1916
p 3

Place	Date	Hour	Summary of Events and Information	Remarks and references to Appendices
LA CLYTTE	JUNE		Sub-sections:- A1, A2, B1, B2, C1, C2, D1, D2. Owing to shortage of iron girders, work on dug-outs and emplacements arrested.	
	19th		MONDAY Enemy machine guns silenced by our 18-pounders.	
	20th		TUESDAY New field found for transport lines. This was necessitated by the proximity of an R.E. dump to the present lines. Situation normal.	
	21st		WEDNESDAY New horse-shelter started.	
	22nd		THURSDAY Intn. section relief. Situation quiet. 2 Lieut Jenvick took over Command of B section.	
	23rd		FRIDAY Situation normal	
	24th		SATURDAY Increased activity from our artillery, causing much damage to enemy's wire. Enemy's retaliation weak.	
	25th		SUNDAY Increased activity from both sides. BOIS CARRÉ shelled. 2 Lieut Ainley knocked down by concussion of bursting shell but continued to carry on his duties very efficiently. 2 Lieut McLeod returned from hospital.	
	26th		MONDAY Enemy's wire systematically broken by shell fire. Retaliation weak. 150th Inf. Brigade carried out a raid on enemy's advanced trench. Enemy's observation balloons	

WAR DIARY 151 BDE MACHINE GUN COMPANY
or
INTELLIGENCE SUMMARY.
Volume 5.
June 1916
Army Form C. 2118.

P4

Place	Date	Hour	Summary of Events and Information	Remarks and references to Appendices
LA CLYTTE	JUNE 27th		destroyed by bombs from aeroplanes.	
	28th		Inter section relief. Enemy's trenches bombarded apparently on large frontage with shells and trench-mortars. LIEUT BROCK appointed adjutant of 50th Division Young Officers School. Bombardment of enemy's trenches continues. Retaliation weak. Spurts of men in trenches high. Three raids carried out by 24th Division on our right	
	29th		Bombardment continues. Raids carried out by 24th Division. Enemy retaliated fiercely on frontage of 149th Inf. Brigade.	
	30th		Enemy very quiet. Preparations for a British offensive in this area continued.	

W Johnston Capt. Company
151 BDE
C'y.

Army Form C. 2118.

50

WAR DIARY
or
INTELLIGENCE SUMMARY

(*Erase heading not required.*)

Vol 2

151st. Machine Gun Company.
War Diary.
July, 1916.
Volume No. 6.

Army Form C. 2118.

WAR DIARY 151st Brigade Machine Gun Company
INTELLIGENCE SUMMARY.
July 1916 Vol 6. P1

(Erase heading not required.)

Place	Date	Hour	Summary of Events and Information	Remarks and references to Appendices
LA CLYTTE	1st		SATURDAY Trench mortar duel on front line trenches during which we gained the superiority. British artillery very active on the whole front. Support of heavy artillery was liberally applied to allow superiority to remain with us. 2149 Pte Dresson promoted to the rank of lance corporal for gallantry under shell fire. British and French offensive commenced North and South of River SOMME.	
	2nd		SUNDAY Situation quiet. Enemy at one period commenced using trench mortars but was silenced by a 12 inch Howitzer on KEMMEL HILL.	
	3rd		MONDAY Situation quiet. Weather oppressively hot. All ranks in the Trenches were in excellent spirits.	
	4th		TUESDAY Situation quiet. Enemy ventured to resume the firing of trench mortars. Our retaliation was severe and effective.	
	5th		WEDNESDAY Enemy more active. Our retaliation on his front line and supports was heavy.	

WAR DIARY or INTELLIGENCE SUMMARY

Army Form C. 2118.

151st Brigade Machine Gun Company

July 1916 Vol 6

Place	Date	Hour	Summary of Events and Information	Remarks and references to Appendices
LA CLYTTE	6th		THURSDAY Gaps made in enemy's wire by our 18-pounders.	
	7th		FRIDAY Situation quiet. Our artillery occasionally fired on the enemy's wire entanglements.	
	8th		SATURDAY Situation unchanged. As a result of reference made in the Allied offensive at the SOMME, activities chiefly was reduced on all telephone messages to and from positions within 1000 yards of enemy's trenches.	
	9th		SUNDAY Intersection relief. Heavy trench mortar shoal on M and N trenches. 2270 Pte Hendersy, D section, wounded. The 6th Durham L.I. sent out a raiding party after dusk with the object of taking a prisoner. After the party had nearly reached the enemy's wire, a trench mortar was attached and one man was captured. The object of the raid being accomplished the raiding party returned immediately	
	10th		MONDAY Situation unchanged.	
	11th		TUESDAY Situation normal. Preparations made for gas and ammonal to be sent from O and P Trenches. Operations postponed	

WAR DIARY or INTELLIGENCE SUMMARY

Army Form C. 2118.

151 Bde. Machine Gun Company

July 1916 Vol. 6 p 3

Place	Date	Hour	Summary of Events and Information	Remarks and references to Appendices
LA CLYTTE	12th		WEDNESDAY Situation quiet. Operations arranged for previous night again postponed.	
	13th		THURSDAY Heavy trench mortar duel between opposing front lines commenced at noon. No casualties. A Raid was arranged by the 8th Durham Light Infy. (leaving N 2 trench) at midnight. The raid was unsuccessful. Intersection relief completed by midnight.	
	14th		FRIDAY N1 emplacement hit by a trench-mortal bomb, part of the front being carried away. The gun was undamaged and emplacement rebuilt during the night.	
	15th		SATURDAY Maxim gun belonging to D Section hit by bullet in their emplacement 02. At 11.30 p.m. enemy made bombing raid on D4 but did not reach the trench. One dead German was brought in on following morning.	
	16th		SUNDAY Machine Gun Company relieved by 149 Brigade Machine Gun Company. A and D sections under 2 Lieut. T.H. Raike went in reserve to 150th Inf. Bde at LOCRE, N 24 d 3.7.	

WAR DIARY

151st Bde. Machine Gun Company.

INTELLIGENCE SUMMARY. p 4

July 1916 Vol 1

Army Form C. 2118.

Place	Date	Hour	Summary of Events and Information	Remarks and references to Appendices
BOESCHAEPE	18th		The remainder of the company who were in Divisional Reserve at N8 c 5.9 (Sheet 27). A programme of training who known up to cover 12 days. Billets were very comfortable and surrounding country very suitable for training in open warfare.	
			TUESDAY Inspection of guns and accessories. Four guns in reserve to 150th Inf. Bde. ordered to POLKA to give covering fire during raid on enemy's trench North of SPANBROEKMOLEN	
	19th		WEDNESDAY at 11.30 a.m. orders were received to relieve 17th Bde. M.G. Company (24th Division) at during the following night in Sector KEMMEL-WYTSCHAETE Rd to D5 inclusive. Relief completed during the night. B section occupied FRENCHMAN'S FARM, MINE SHAFT, BATTLE AXE, KINGSWAY. C section occupied S.P.8 (2 positions), S.P.9, and S.P.10. S.P.8 was in a bad state of repair and the right gun being superfluous steps were immediately taken for its withdrawal. One gun of D section occupied FORT REGINA. 7 guns were in Brigade Reserve at BEAVER HALL N31 a 9.5. Divisional front extended from O4 to D5 inclusive	

WAR DIARY or **INTELLIGENCE SUMMARY**

Army Form C. 2118.

151 Brigade Machine Gun Company

July 1916 Vol 6 p 5

Place	Date	Hour	Summary of Events and Information	Remarks and references to Appendices
KEMMEL HILL	20th		THURSDAY The general situation for this sector is quiet, though the enemy at times makes the front line very uncomfortable with trench mortars and at nighttime the open ground behind the trenches with rifle and machine gun fire.	
	21st		FRIDAY New position sighted and open emplacement built for emplacements guns in SP.8.	
	22nd		SATURDAY 3 guns moved from Brigade Reserve at BEAVER HALL to positions in new extension of line to C.4 — Vis CELLIA, S.P.11a, and S.P.11. S.P.11 deemed practically useless on account of the very limited field of fire. Work commenced on new and strong dug-out for machine gun officer in REGENT STREET. 6 s.a.p. manned with 8 feet earth for over head cover commenced for protection of detachment in S.P.9 was commenced. Stratos normal.	
	23rd		SUNDAY Work on a range for machine guns commenced at BEAVER HALL narrow road approaching to BEAVER HALL was repaired by section. Strong dug-out commenced for detachment at BATTLE AXE position.	

WAR DIARY
151st Brigade Machine Gun Company Army Form C. 2118
INTELLIGENCE SUMMARY.

July 1916 p.6

Place	Date	Hour	Summary of Events and Information	Remarks and references to Appendices
KEMMEL HILL	24th		MONDAY Situation continued to be normal. 2 Lieut. E.S. Jackson (Sergt. 8th D.L.I. attd. 151 Bde. M.G. Company) commenced duty as a Commissioned officer with the Company. Open alternative emplacement made at KINGSWAY.	
	25th		TUESDAY Situation normal. Work commenced on strong dug-out (cement roof with girders) for detachment at MINE SHAFT emplacement.	
	26th		WEDNESDAY Situation normal. Direct telephone communication opened out to officer i/c right group. 149 Inf. Bde. extended the sector held by them northwards up to and including the BULL RING. Enemy trench mortars on left Battalion front. Such operations of the enemy invariably cease when retaliation can be gained from the heavy artillery, but the process is a long one.	
	27th		THURSDAY A subsection ordered to be continually attached to Battalion in Divisional Reserve at WAKEFIELD HUTS under orders from the C.O. of the Battalion.	

WAR DIARY
or
INTELLIGENCE SUMMARY.

Army Form C. 2118.

151st Bde Machine Gun Company.

July 1916
p 7.

Place	Date	Hour	Summary of Events and Information	Remarks and references to Appendices
KEMMEL HILL	28th		FRIDAY Situation normal. Heavy artillery were ready to give immediate retaliation to enemy should he commence his customary murderous bombardment. Unfortunately the enemy remained quiet. Indirect fire from new positions commenced after dark.	
	29th		SATURDAY Headquarters and transport ordered to move at short notice. Move was delayed for 3 hours by enemy observation balloon. Headquarters and transport were in new area M.4.d.3.8. by 6 p.m. Weather very hot.	
	30th		SUNDAY Situation very quiet. The weather was very hot. 151st Bde Machine Gun Company in future to be called 151st Machine Gun Company. Sap in S.P.9 completed, also dug-out with cement roof at MINE SHAFT position, both shewed withstand a direct hit from a 5.9" shell.	
	31st		MONDAY Situation quiet. Indirect fire from near PDKA and FRENCHMAN'S FARM brought to bear respectively on WYTSCHAETE and enemy communications to PECKHAM.	

W.A. Hutton Capt.
C.O. 151st Machine Gun Company

"31.7.16. Positions occupied by 151st Machine Gun Company, East of Kemmel."

1. Vn Gellia
2. S P 11
3. S P 11 a
4. Ft Regent
5. S P 10
6. Fm D'Hono
7. S P 9
8. S P 8
9. Mine Shaft
10. Frenchmans Farm
A. Spy Farm
B. Ft Regent

Army Form C. 2118.

WAR DIARY
or
INTELLIGENCE SUMMARY

(Erase heading not required.)

War Diary
of
151st Machine Gun Company

August 1916

Vol 3

Volume No X

VOLUME 7 PAGE 1

MACHINE GUN COMPANY

AUGUST 1916

WAR DIARY
or
INTELLIGENCE SUMMARY.

Army Form C. 2118.

Place	Date	Hour	Summary of Events and Information	Remarks and references to Appendices
REMMEL	1st		Tuesday. "C" Section relieved "D" Section. Work commenced and good progress made with cap. for VIA GELLIA emplacement. Normal situation generally except of a Trench Mortar duel during the early evening	
	2nd		Wednesday. Situation normal. 2 LT V. COX to hospital with attack of malaria.	
	3rd		Thursday. Normal. Definite orders that the Division will move south.	
	4th		Friday. B" Section made good progress with caps in S.P. 8 & 9. Indirect fire at after on WYTSCHAETE and enemy C.T.'s to PECKHAM.	
	5th		Saturday. D" Section relieved B" Section. The 149th Brigade (on our left) had an artillery strafe, to which there was a heavy retaliation, but we suffered no casualties	
	6th		Sunday. Everything quiet. Work on cap. in VIA GELLIA emplacement arrested through water. 56th MACHINE GUN COMPANY arrived from the SOMME. Bristol aeroplane very active	
	7th		Officers of the 56th M.G.C toured Kemmel. Detachments of ours at left and FRENCHMAN'S FARM relieved by 57th M.G.C.	
	8th		Company was relieved in 3 p.m. without casualties in spite of heavy hostile artillery fire	
	9th		Inspection of Company in full marching order.	

VOLUME 7. PAGE 2.

151st MACHINE GUN COMPANY

AUGUST WAR DIARY 1916

INTELLIGENCE SUMMARY.

Army Form C. 2118.

Place	Date	Hour	Summary of Events and Information	Remarks and references to Appendices
KEMMEL	10th		Thursday. Company paraded to march to BOESCHAEPE at 9.45 p.m. Wagons, horses and mules entrained without incident.	
CANDAS	11th		Friday. Train left BOESCHAEPE at 1.15 a.m. arriving at CANDAS at 10 a.m. The Company then marched 9 miles to RIBAUCOURT. The men marched well. Billets were in poor condition, but surrounding country excellent.	
RIBAUCOURT	12th		Saturday. Preparations made for a course of training.	
	13th		Sunday. Weather cooler.	
	14th		Monday. Squad Drill in morning. Preparations made for further move.	
VIGNACOURT	15th		Company marched with Brigade through DOMART-en-PONTHIEU, ST LEGER, BERTEINCOURT arriving at VIGNACOURT at 10.30 a.m. The Company marched well.	
BAIZIEUX	16th		Wednesday. The Brigade left VIGNACOURT at 7.0 a.m. and marched through MOUFLERS-AU-BOIS to BAIZIEUX WOOD. 10 tents were allotted to the Company in BAIZIEUX WOOD. The men made bivouacs with TA-HILL. 36 Machine gun Coy, attached 2nd in command of 151st M.G.C. Lt A.M. GELSTHORPE, 2nd in command 151st M.G.C, attached to command 76th M.G.C. 2 Lt H.W. MAY joined Company from Machine Gun Corps Base Depot as Transport Officer	

W.H. Hastings Capt
151 M.G.C

VOLUME 7 PAGES 3   151st MACHINE GUN COMPANY

AUGUST WAR DIARY 1916

INTELLIGENCE SUMMARY.

(Erase heading not required.)

Army Form C. 2118.

Place	Date	Hour	Summary of Events and Information	Remarks and references to Appendices
BAIZIEUX	17th		Thursday. Equipment thoroughly overhauled.	
	18th 19th		Friday Saturday. These days were spent in preliminary training.	
	-20th		Captain A.M. GELSTHORPE departed for the new command	
	21st		Lt. T.A. HILL arrived from the 36th M.G.C.	
	22nd -to- 21-28		2nd Lt. J.W. BRADDELL joined the company from Machine gun Corps Base Depot. This period was spent in the Company in physical training, and practice of offensive operations in kilted and open warfare. An excellent system of training was devised, on which all sections had a thorough training. On the 27th, heavy rain set in, and continued for several days.	
	29th		This day was set apart for a Brigade attack scheme, but heavy rains caused operations to be cancelled.	
	30th		The Brigade scheme of the previous day was carried out. The Company had 8 guns covering the attack. 4 guns in reserve, & 4 guns advancing with attacking party. Rain shortened operations. 2nd Lt. MACLEOD departed on transfer, to the 12th (Labour) Bn Royal Highlanders.	
	31st		Day spent in overhauling equipment. Derived improvement in weather.	

Supplement to War Diary of
151 Machine Gun Company.   p1

Formation of Company.

The 151 Machine Gun Company was formed by order of the 50 Division on February 6th 16. and was composed of the Machine Gun Sections of the following Battalions.

6th Bn. Durh. L.I.
8" " " "
9" " " "
5" Border Regt.

Nominal Roll of Officers.—

Capt.	W.O. Grierson. Cmdg.	detached from	5th N. Lancs.
Lieut.	A. M. Gelsthorpe 2d in Command	"	8th Bn. Durh. L.I.
"	A. L. Brock.	"	6" " " "
"	R. W. Marley.	"	5" Border Regt.
"	H. E. Wood.	"	" " " "
2 Lieut.	J. A. G. Ainley	"	6" Bn. Durh. L.I.
"	A. M. Jones.	"	8" " " "
"	H. G. Allison.	"	9" " " "
"	L. E. Tomlinson.	"	9" " " "
1869	C.S.M. J. Malpass.	"	6" " " "
1011	C.Q.M.S. A. Suddlin.	"	9" " " "

Notes on Establishment.

The Establishment of a Bde. M/Gun Company only allows for 4 men per gun with the addition of one N.C.O. per gun.

The 16 privates on Headquarters as Range Takers and scouts, had to be employed as grooms, pioneers etc and to replace sick in gun numbers, in order to keep 4 men on each gun. This has been proved to be quite

2

inadequate for stationary warfare, where much work on emplacements and dugouts is required to be done, and rations to be carried up, etc.

I consider six men per gun is the minimum necessary.

I should recommend also, the following additions to establishment:-

One transport officer,
One skilled Armourer Sergeant.
12 Signallers.
1 travelling Field Kitchen, and a 2nd G.S. wagon for baggage.

1.8.16.

W.A.Grierson
Captain.
Cmdg 151 Machine Gun Company.

151st. INFANTRY BRIGADE
50th. DIVISION

151st. MACHINE GUN COMPANY

SEPTEMBER 1916.

Army Form C. 2118.

WAR DIARY
or
INTELLIGENCE SUMMARY.
(Erase heading not required.)

Vol 4

CONFIDENTIAL

WAR DIARY
of
151 MACHINE GUN COMPANY

FROM 1st SEPT 1916 TO 30th SEPT. 1916.

VOLUME Nº 8.

CONFIDENTIAL

Army Form C. 2118.

WAR DIARY OF 1st MACHINE GUN COMPANY

or

INTELLIGENCE SUMMARY.

(Erase heading not required.)

VOLUME 8
PAGE 1
SEPT 1st 1916 to Sept 30 1916

Place	Date	Hour	Summary of Events and Information	Remarks and references to Appendices
BAIZIEUX	Sept 2nd 3rd		These days were spent in leaving the company in various modes of progression under fire, also in consolidating captured trenches. The Company formed in a brigade practice attack on trenches near GRANVILLERS CONTAY ROAD. 4 guns were sent across with the attack, 4 guns across to and overlook fire, 4 went inward. The other 4 remained in reserve.	
	4th 5th 6th		All sections were given a thorough practice on the range. Kits & equipment were thoroughly overhauled. Sections were placed at the disposal of the battalion commanders for practice in open warfare.	
	7th 8th		The practice attack of the 3rd September was repeated. The morning was spent in a general overhauling. From 7 p.m. till 1 a.m. next morning the sections were in turn listed or firing at unknown targets (on flare lights alone). The men had to rely on their own observation & much valuable experience under the conditions of a counter attack by night was gained.	
	9th		The Company paraded in an open order attack on a lightly entrenched position	

B. Huijsmans
OC 1st MGC

CONFIDENTIAL

Army Form C. 2118.

Instructions regarding War Diaries and Intelligence
Summaries are contained in F. S. Regs., Part II.
and the Staff Manual respectively. Title pages
will be prepared in manuscript.

WAR DIARY of 151st M.G.C.
or
INTELLIGENCE SUMMARY.
(Erase heading not required.)

SEPT 1st to 30th 1916

VOLUME 8 PAGE 2

Place	Date	Hour	Summary of Events and Information	Remarks and references to Appendices
BAIZIEUX	9th		The Vickers guns on this occasion proved most conspicuous from the Lewis rifles. Thanks to the special training our men received rather elsewhere. In the evening the general worked in and had an informal reception, and was given an opportunity of critisizing the various methods devised of carrying the gun and its accessories.	
BECOURT	10th		The company moved at 7.15 am to BECOURT WOOD via HENENCOURT and ALBERT. Here all ranks bivouacked.	
	11th		The Company lived in BECOURT WOOD.	
	12th 10th-14th		At 7.30 p.m. the Company moved forward to the S.W corner of MAMETZ WOOD, but contain gunners, one N°1 on N°2 from each team were left behind at the transport to serve as trained & experienced nucleus in the event of any untoward occurence to the company	
MAMETZ WOOD	15th		at 6 p.m. two teams of "A" Section were sent to JUTLAND AVENUE	
			3113 Pte Charlton W.form was wounded on the way up.	
QUARRY	16th		At 2 a.m the remainder of the company proceeded to its new Headquarters at the QUARRY N.E of BAZENTIN - LE - PETIT, and	

CONFIDENTIAL

Army Form C. 2118.

Instructions regarding War Diaries and Intelligence Summaries are contained in F. S. Regs., Part II. and the Staff Manual respectively. Title pages will be prepared in manuscript.

WAR DIARY of 15th M.G.C.

or

INTELLIGENCE SUMMARY.

(Erase heading not required.)

SEPT 1st to 30th 1916   VOLUME 6   PAGES

Place	Date	Hour	Summary of Events and Information	Remarks and references to Appendices
QUARRY	16th		relieved the 149th M.G.C. The remaining two guns of "B" section both up a further in the German old front line. The layers of "D" section were placed in positions near the QUARRY to carry out indirect fire. Two guns of "B" section were sent into the SWITCH LINE	
	17th		2nd Lt ALLISON H.E., 9th D.L.I. att'd M.G.C. was wounded in the premature burst from an 18-pounder gun behind the Quarry. This gun did great execution among our own men during the day	
	18th 19th		During several attacks by our troops & one from plantation, the enemy support & communication trenches were constantly attacks on. There two days, our guns plastered the enemy support & communication trenches In all during the 15th 17th 18th 19th over 30,000 rounds were fired 27154 Pte WARREN A. and 17630 Pte ORR both of the Machine gun Corps were wounded	
MAMETZ WOOD	20th 21st 22nd 23rd -27		The Company was relieved by the 149th M.G.C, and returned to the S.W. corner of MAMETZ WOOD, where they remained for 3 days The Company went forward in support of the Brigade in support & moved forward to the NW corner of MAMETZ WOOD, where they remained for 5 days	

CONFIDENTIAL

Army Form C. 2118.

WAR DIARY of 150TH M.G.C.

INTELLIGENCE SUMMARY. from Sept 1st to Sept 30 1916 VOLUME 8 PAGE 64

(Erase heading not required.)

Instructions regarding War Diaries and Intelligence Summaries are contained in F. S. Regs., Part II. and the Staff Manual respectively. Title pages will be prepared in manuscript.

Place	Date	Hour	Summary of Events and Information	Remarks and references to Appendices
MAMETZ WOOD	26th–27th		Six guns, half of "A" Section were sent to cover the 150th Brigade attack but covering fire. On this occasion there was no artillery preparation, but to role barrage employed up to the Zero hour was maintained by 18 machine Guns. Our guns remained in the line till our infantry relieved the 150th M.G.C.	
	27th 28th		The 2nd Lt. J.C.M [?] joined the company from the Base Depot. The Company relieved the 150th M.G.C. with Headquarters at QUARRY. Three guns of "A" Section were placed in or around PRUE COPSE, 3 the in STARFISH TRENCH. In the former place its outgoing company had afforded been wont to walk & stand about in the open in clear & close view of the enemy. Consequently the place came in for a good deal of attention from hostile artillery. "D" Section were placed in RUTHERFORD ALLEY where they could maintain indirect fire on FAVCOURT ABBAYE and LE SARS. "B" section were out to the left of our divisional line and took up a position to prevent any attack from the left flank, at which	

T/2134. W. W708-776. 500000. 4/15. Sir J. C. & S.

CONFIDENTIAL

Army Form C. 2118.

WAR DIARY of 115th M.G.C.
or
INTELLIGENCE SUMMARY.

from Sept 1st to Sept 30th 1916

VOLUME 8
Pp 6-E 5.

Instructions regarding War Diaries and Intelligence Summaries are contained in F. S. Regs., Part II. and the Staff Manual respectively. Title pages will be prepared in manuscript.

(Erase heading not required.)

Place	Date	Hour	Summary of Events and Information	Remarks and references to Appendices
SUMMARY	28th		Joint had muses considerable of the next division "Q" Section remained in reserve	
	29th		See Lt. P.H. JENRICH was wounded by shrapnel. At 6 p.m. the Bavarians were probable to attack a portion of the FLERS LINE, but met a large counter-attack. The guns of "B" Section & "D" Section found with the attack most moved fire on the enemy seen N.E. of EAUCOURT L'ABBAYE which made the enemy more frantic. There was open in making preparation for the next operations	
	30th			

[signature] Major
115th M.G. Battalion
O.C.

War Diary

October 1916

151 Machine Gun Coy

Volume No 4.

WAR DIARY or INTELLIGENCE SUMMARY

Army Form C. 2118.
VOLUME 9   PAGE 1

Place	Date	Hour	Summary of Events and Information	Remarks and references to Appendices
TRENCHES NEAR EAUCOURT L'ABBAYE	OCT 1st		The Brigade attacked the FLERS system of trenches at 3.15 p.m. The artillery preparation took the form of a steady bombardment from 7 a.m. to the Zero hour, and then an intense bombardment. "A", "B", "D" sections remained in their original positions, and "C" Section were ordered to co-operate with the attacking battalions. Two guns went with the 6th D.L.I. who attacked on the right, and two on the left with 8th D.L.I. All 4 guns were in position by dawn. The two right guns under Sgt Foster did not go over with the attack. One was placed off a communication trench and fired towards the right in case the Division on our right failed to reach its objective. This position proved extremely valuable as the neighbouring Division failed to reach its objective, & the enemy held a portion of the trench between the two divisions. The other gun after the armament proved successful were placed in the old GERMAN front line in the FLERS system. The two guns on the left under Sgt J.W. BRADDELL took up a position at dawn close to own bombing block in the communication trench leading to the FLERS line. As the infantry attacked then got out of the trench, & advanced with the infantry into the front line. They were enabled to do this without a single casualty, thanks to the complete unexpectedness of the attack, later Sgt J.W. BRADDELL went to hospital wounded with	

WAR DIARY
or
INTELLIGENCE SUMMARY.
(Erase heading not required.)

Army Form C. 2118.

Place	Date	Hour	Summary of Events and Information	Remarks and references to Appendices
TRENCHES NEAR EAUCOURT L'ABBAYE	Oct 1st		about dark, 2nd A.M. JONES who was in charge of "B" section, now learning that Mr BRADSHAW was incapacitated, in spite of a badly injured foot, hastened across into the captured trenches and organized the position. Meanwhile Corporals BUTTER and DIGGLE in charge of their two guns had done excellent work reconnoitring the newly captured trenches and finding & improving their new positions.	
	2nd		On the night of Oct 2nd & 3rd the Company were due to be relieved by the 119th M.G.C. and to return to a position in support in HOOK TRENCH. This was done with all except "C" Section, two of this relieving teams incurring several casualties when on the way to relieve them. They were eventually relieved on the afternoon of the 3rd.	
	3rd		PTES WELHAN and WOLSTENHOLME were killed by a 5.9 shell. L.C. LEFTLEY, in charge of the right forward gun of "C" Section went alone over a double bombing block and captured and brought in 22 prisoners, Germans.	
	4th		In the morning the Company was relieved by the Coy and returned to BECOURT WOOD. The Company moved next the rest of the Brigade to HENENCOURT WOOD	

Army Form C. 2118.

WAR DIARY
or
INTELLIGENCE SUMMARY.
(Erase heading not required.)

Instructions regarding War Diaries and Intelligence Summaries are contained in F. S. Regs., Part II. and the Staff Manual respectively. Title pages will be prepared in manuscript.

Place	Date	Hour	Summary of Events and Information	Remarks and references to Appendices
ETENEHEM	Oct 5th-20th		This period was spent in cleaning & replenishing kits and equipment. All sections were given plenty of practice on the range. Footballs were procured & many exciting games were played between the various sections.	
	12th		2Lt G.V Cox rejoined the Company from the HS 12 M.G.C.	
	13th		2Lt. A.M Jones to 25th M.G.C as 2nd in-command	
	14th		2Lt R.E. Landels joined the Company from CAMIERS.	
	15th		2Lt Th Reade, Ptes Robley and Mason proceeded to CAMIERS on an advanced M.G. Course.	
	17th		2Lt. E.S. Jackson to hospital with badly sprained ankle.	
	20th		Cpl Diggle and Cpl Butler awarded Military Medal for excellent work on Oct 1st	
	21st		A practice of a counter attack by night prove most interesting and instructive. A sudden drop in temperature enabled us to obtain insight experience in the best means of ensuring the warmth & firing of the guns in cold weather.	
	23rd		The Company moved to the W. of BECOURT WOOD, & encamped in the No Man's ...	

Army Form C. 2118.

WAR DIARY
or
INTELLIGENCE SUMMARY.
(Erase heading not required.)

Instructions regarding War Diaries and Intelligence Summaries are contained in F. S. Regs., Part II. and the Staff Manual respectively. Title pages will be prepared in manuscript.

Place	Date	Hour	Summary of Events and Information	Remarks and references to Appendices
BECOURT	Oct 23rd		2nd of July, 2Lt. A.M. JONES was awarded the MILITARY CROSS.	
	24th		A very rainy day.	
	25th		The Company moved to E of MAMETZ WOOD, forming part of the Brigade in reserve, and relieving 27th M.G.C. The ground was extremely greasy, and we were extremely fortunate to arrive without mishap to our transport.	
	26th		2Lt T.H. READE proceeded to ENGLAND on receipt of word from GRANTHAM	
	27th		2Lt V.C.B. HILL joined the Company from CAMIERS.	
	28th – 31st		The Company remained in Brigade reserve, and spent an uninteresting time watching the rain fall, & trying to remain from or its feet in a sea of mud.	

W.G. Ficuson
Major
Cmdg 151 MGCom(pany)

Army Form C. 2118.

Vol 6

WAR DIARY
or
INTELLIGENCE SUMMARY.
(Erase heading not required.)

CONFIDENTIAL.

WAR DIARY

OF

151 MACHINE GUN COMPANY.

FOR MONTH OF NOVEMBER 1916.
(1ST to 30TH November 1916)

VOLUME No 10.

Army Form C. 2118.

War Diary of 151 M.G.C.
Page No 1.

WAR. DIARY
or
INTELLIGENCE SUMMARY.
(Erase heading not required.)

Place	Date	Hour	Summary of Events and Information	Remarks and references to Appendices
In the Field	1916. Nov. 1st to 3rd		In Divisional reserve at CATERPILLAR VALLEY, East of MAMETZ WOOD. Officers and N.C.O.s reconnoitred approaches to the line.	
In trenches near Butte de WARLENCOURT	3/4th		On the night of 3/4th the Company relieved 149th M.G.C. in the right Sub Sector of the Divisional Front and 150th M.G.C. on the left Sub Sector. All 16 guns of the Company occupied fixed positions.	
	4th		Operation orders received for attack on BUTTE DE WARLENCOURT. GIRD LINE. Opposite Divisional Front; by 151.I.Bde, supported by 2 Batts of 149th I. Bde. 8 m/guns of 149th M.G.C. attached for indirect fire.	
	5th		The 151. I. Bde attacked at 9.10 a.m. 2 guns of "B" Section were attached to left Batt = (9th D.L.I.) 2 guns of "B" Section were attached to centre Batt = (6th D.L.I.) and 2 guns of "D" Section were	

WAR DIARY
or
INTELLIGENCE SUMMARY.

Army Form C. 2118.

PAGE No. 2.

attached to right Batln. = (8' D.L.I). The left Batln. alone reached its objective and captured the BUTTE DE WARLENCOURT. Corporal Rutherford - 'B' Section established his gun in a post on the NORTH side of the BAPAUME road. He and all his team became casualties. This gun is missing. Corporal Mowed's gun 'B' Section (2ⁿᵈ gun attached to left Batln.) was every shot but J action and replaced by Corporal Watson. Gun J 'A' Section, as both flanks of left Batln. were in the air - Sergt. Clennell's gun 'A' Section and Corporal Butler's gun 'C' Section were sent up to hold left flank. These 3 guns did extremely good work - repelling the first counter attack by the Germans early in the night. In the second counter attack which took place about 11 p.m. the 3 guns kept in action, firing hard until troops flanking had been surrounded by enemy bombers, when the 3 guns were forced to be withdrawn, the teams suffering very heavy casualties.

Army Form C. 2118.

WAR DIARY
or
INTELLIGENCE SUMMARY.
(Erase heading not required.)

PAGE 3.

Place	Date	Hour	Summary of Events and Information	Remarks and references to Appendices
			The 2 guns of "B" Section attached to Centre Batt. went forward with the 3rd wave, but the Battalion was held up by MyGun fire, and the 2 guns were stranded in NO MANS LAND. Sergeant Leith's gun was knocked out and acc its detachment with the exception of Private Middlemas who did excellent work getting the wounded back to our old front line. Private Skey took charge of this gun when the N.C.O. was killed and brought his gun back to our old front line, where he kept it in action all day supported by only one other man. 2 guns of "D" Section went forward with the right Blank, and 2nd Lieut LANDELS, R.E. were also held up, but here withdrawn from NO MANS LAND during the day with slight casualties.	
	6/7.		6/7 - by the 150th M.G.C. and returned to former position	

WAR DIARY
or
INTELLIGENCE SUMMARY.
(Erase heading not required.)

Army Form C. 2118.

Page No: 4

Place	Date	Hour	Summary of Events and Information	Remarks and references to Appendices
	11th		As Divisional Reserve near Mametz Wood. List of Casualties during the action are given in Appendix II.	
			5" Guns under 2nd Lieut. G.S. Hervey were sent up to man the line of M/Gun nests laid out as an intermediate line in the 3rd Corps defence scheme, 500 yards South of EAUCOURT L'ABAYE.	
	14th		The G.O.C. 151 I. Bde. inspected M/Gun nests, accompanied by O.C. 151 M.G.C.	
	16th		5" Guns in M/Gun nests relieved and returned to Company near Mametz Wood. 151 I. Bde relieved by 3rd I. Bde - 1st Division.	
	17th		The Company marched back to MILLENCOURT, starting	

Army Form C. 2118.

WAR DIARY
or
INTELLIGENCE SUMMARY.
(Erase heading not required.)

Page No 5

Place	Date	Hour	Summary of Events and Information	Remarks and references to Appendices
	18th to 30th		at 9.00 a.m. and was billeted in old barns in the village. This period was spent in training the recruits received reinforcements in stoppages etc. Permanent working parties had to be found daily by the rear of the Company for the IV Corps Rest Station.	
	30th		Operation orders received to move back to WARLOY on the 1st December 1916.	
			APPENDIX I – Reinforcements Received. " II – Casualties. " III – List of Honours awarded during the month.	

[signature] [signature]
Capt 15th M.G. Coy.

Army Form C. 2118.

APPENDIX I

WAR DIARY
or
INTELLIGENCE SUMMARY.
(Erase heading not required.)

Instructions regarding War Diaries and Intelligence Summaries are contained in F. S. Regs., Part II. and the Staff Manual respectively. Title pages will be prepared in manuscript.

Place	Date 1916 Nov	Hour	Summary of Events and Information	Remarks and references to Appendices
In the Field			REINFORCEMENTS RECEIVED DURING NOVEMBER.	
	2		1 OR from No.1 A.S.C. Section advanced Horse Transport Depot	
	8		2nd Lt Hervey G.S. from M.G. Corps Base Depot	
	10		2nd Lt Butler L.R. do	
	11		20 – ORs do	
	12		9 – ORs do	
	12		2nd Lt Graham J.P. do	
	16		2nd Lt Hill P.C. do	
	16		1 – OR do	
	21		10 ORs do	
	22		2nd Lt Lewis H do	

WAR DIARY
or
INTELLIGENCE SUMMARY.

Army Form C. 2118. Appendix II

Place	Date	Hour	Summary of Events and Information	Remarks and references to Appendices
In the field.	1916 Nov.		CASUALTIES &c DURING NOVEMBER	
	3.		2nd Lt Hill C.V.B. — To hospital sick	
	4.		2 — ORs — wounded in action.	
	5.		2nd Lt Cox G.V. — wounded in action.	
			1 — OR — killed in action.	
			9 — ORs — wounded in action	
			2 — ORs — missing	
	6.		1 — OR — wounded and missing	
	8.		1 — OR — wounded in action	
	9.		2nd Lt Lisgo J.C.N. — To hospital sick	
			2nd Lt Landels R.E — do	

Army Form C. 2118.

WAR DIARY
or
INTELLIGENCE SUMMARY.

Appendix (VII)

(Erase heading not required.)

Place	Date	Hour	Summary of Events and Information	Remarks and references to Appendices
In the field	1916 Nov. 20		LIST OF HONOURS & AWARDS	
		Reg No.		
		24302	Sergt. Clennell J.W. — M.G.C.	
		24287	Cpl. Watson T.M. — do —	MILITARY MEDAL for bravery in the field
		10023	Pte. Hoy J.C. — do —	
		24323	" Middlemas W. — do —	
		36771	" Jones W.T. — do —	
		3849	" Dickinson A. 9th D.L.I. — att. Carrying Party	

Vol 7

WAR DIARY
151st Machine Gun Company
30th November
to
31st December.

VOLUME No XI

WAR DIARY
or
INTELLIGENCE SUMMARY.
(Erase heading not required.)

Army Form C. 2118.

Page 1.

Place	Date	Hour	Summary of Events and Information	Remarks and references to Appendices
In the Field.	December 1st		The Company moved from MILLENCOURT to WARLOY.	
	3rd to 9th		TRAINING. 1st Period. Section Training.	
	11th–16th		— do — 2nd " Company Training.	
	18th–23rd		— do — 3rd " Advanced Company Training.	
	25th		Xmas Day.	
	26th & 27th		Brigade Training. 4 Sections of the Company working in conjunction with respective Battalions.	
	28th		The Company moved from WARLOY to ALBERT.	
	29th		A & B Sections moved from ALBERT to HIGH WOOD EAST CAMP.	
			Reconnaissance of gun positions in the line by O.C. and the 2 Section Officers.	
	30/31		Night of A & B Sections relieved 2 sections of 2nd M.G.C. in the line.	
	31st		The Company (less 2 sections) moved from ALBERT to HIGH WOOD EAST CAMP. Casualties during month – NIL.	WH

Army Form C. 2118.

WAR DIARY
or
INTELLIGENCE SUMMARY.
(Erase heading not required.)

Original

Vol 8

CONFIDENTIAL.

WAR DIARY

OF

151 MACHINE GUN COMPANY.

FROM 1ST JANUARY 1917
TO
31ST JANUARY 1917.

VOLUME XII

Army Form C. 2118.

WAR DIARY
or
INTELLIGENCE SUMMARY.
(Erase heading not required.)

Page 1.

151 Machine Gun Company

Place	Date	Hour	Summary of Events and Information	Remarks and references to Appendices
In the Field	1917. JAN 1st		In trenches near GUEUDECOURT. "A" and "B" Sections in the line; "C" and "D" Sections in Reserve in HIGH WOOD EAST CAMP.	
	NIGHT OF 3/4"		"C" Section relieved "A" Section.	
	7/8"		"D" " " "B" "	
	11/12"		"A" " " "C" "	
	15/16"		"B" " " "D" "	
	19/20"		"C" " " "A" "	
	23/24"		"D" " " "B" "	
	25/26"		The Company was relieved by 2nd Australian M/Gun Company.	APPENDIX I. APPOINTMENTS CASUALTIES ETC. "
	26"	10 AM	The Company moved to BECOURT CAMP "D".	APPENDIX II. MAP OF POSITIONS ETC
	29"	2.25 p.m.	The Company moved to Billets in RIBEMONT.	
	31st		Commenced 9 days Section training.	
			Each night during period 3rd Jan. to 25th Jan. 3/4000 rounds were fired by the forward Guns on to Hostile roads, tracks and dumps in conjunction with divisional 18 Pounder batteries.	

WAR DIARY
or
INTELLIGENCE SUMMARY.

Army Form C. 2118.

Place	Date	Hour	Summary of Events and Information	Remarks and references to Appendices
	9/1/17		**APPENDIX I** PAGE I. **CASUALTIES** 70418. Pte. Bell. J. wounded in action, whilst carrying timber. **APPOINTMENTS** 2nd Lieut. H.N. MAY appointed 2nd in Command 151st M.G.C. Auth. AG's No. A/15908/150 dated 15/1/1917. 2nd Lt. H.N. May granted leave to England 3rd to 13th Jan. 1917 and was admitted to Millbank Hospital London, sick, leave extended to 21/1/17 by authority of War Office. 2nd Lt. R.E. Landale returned from Hospital 9/1/17. 2nd Lt. R.E. Landale left for 4th Army HQ on 22/1/17 to guide Italian Officers over 4th Army Area.	

APPENDIX I.   PAGE 2

The following proceeded on Course of Training in VICKERS GUN at Machine Gun School, Camiers, on the 14th Janry. 17.

          2 Lt. J.R. Graham.
24360.   Cpl. J. Lucas.
10023.   L/Cpl. J.C. Hoy.
70417.   Pte. J. Meeham.
70404.   "   Hudson.

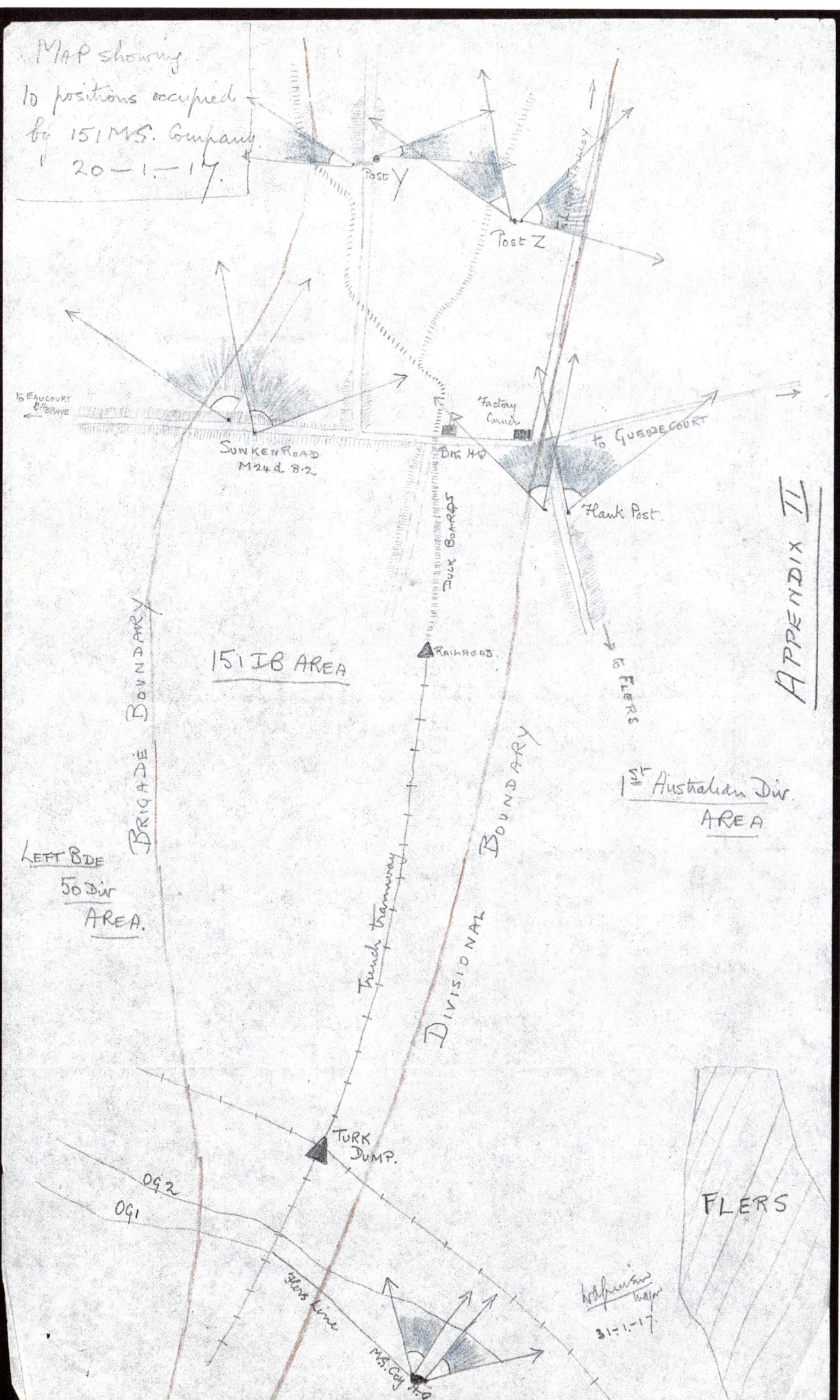

WAR DIARY
or
INTELLIGENCE SUMMARY.

Army Form C. 2118.

CONFIDENTIAL

WAR DIARY

OF

151 MACHINE GUN COY

FROM 1st FEB: 1917 To 28th "   "

VOLUME XII

Vol 9

Reynolds 2 Lieut to.
O.C. 151 M.G.C.

WAR DIARY
or
INTELLIGENCE SUMMARY.

(Erase heading not required.)

Army Form C. 2118.

Page 1.

Place	Date	Hour	Summary of Events and Information	Remarks and references to Appendices
In the Field.	February 1st		AT RIBEMONT.	
	1st to 7th		Training as per programme attached. (Appendix I).	
	8th		2nd Lieut. R.E. LANDELS returned from 4th Army H.Q.	
	8th		2nd " J.G.R. THRUTCHLEY joined as reinforcement from M.G.C. Base Dept.	
	9th		The Company marched to HAMEL en route for FOUCAUCOURT.	
	11th		The Company completed its march to FOUCAUCOURT and was billeted in CAMP CIMETIÈRE in huts which had been evacuated by the French troops.	
	11th to 18th		The Company was in reserve at CAMP CIMETIÈRE, and three sections supplied guns and personnel for anti-aircraft work in intermediate line, and rear position at FOUCAUCOURT.	
	NIGHT 19/20		The Company relieved the 150th M.G.C. in the line, the machine guns being laid chiefly for barrage fire.	
	21st		The O.C. (Major W.A. GRIERSON) developed blood poison in left forefinger and was admitted to Hospital on the 22nd.	
	22nd		2nd Lieut. G.S. HERVEY assumed temporary command of the Company.	DEL

WAR DIARY or INTELLIGENCE SUMMARY

Army Form C. 2118.

Page. 2.

Place	Date	Hour	Summary of Events and Information	Remarks and references to Appendices
	23rd		2nd Lieut. G.S. HERVEY (Acting O.C.) was wounded in action.	
	24th		2nd Lieut. R.E. LANDELS assumed temporary command of the Company. 2nd Lieut. J.C.N. LOW reported for duty. Reinforcement from M.G.C. Base Depot.	
	NIGHT 27/28th		5 guns of the Company assisted in a scheme which was carried out by the Brigade on our left.	
	28th		Lieut. R.L. BAILEY assumed duties of second in command, having been posted from 1st M.G. Coy, and took over temporary Command from 2nd Lt. R.E. LANDELS.	

Reginald Landels 2/Lt.
O.C. 151 M.G.C.

51 M/Gun Coy.

Training Programme. Feb 1st - Feb 8th 1917.

TIME	Saturday 1st	Thursday	Friday	Saturday	Sunday	Monday	Tuesday	Wednesday	Thursday
		2	3		5th	6th	7th	8th	
9 – 9.30	← PHYSICAL DRILL →								
9.30 – 10.15	CLEANING & Overhauling Guns, Belts				INSPECTION OF GUNS				
10.15 – 11.00	Aiming Rests Short exercises Bolt				Rifle Exercises				
11.15 – Noon	Tripod Drill				Close Order Drill				
12.15 – 1.0	Range Attendance				March Route	Belt filling Carry Belt Protecting infantry	Gun Drill	Gun Drill	
					March with Transport	A Section	B Sec	C Sec	D Sec

2/1/17

Army Form C. 2118.

WAR DIARY
~~INTELLIGENCE SUMMARY~~

(Erase heading not required.)

151st Machine Gun Company.

March, 1917.

Volume 14.

Army Form C. 2118.

WAR DIARY
or
INTELLIGENCE SUMMARY.
(Erase heading not required.)

CONFIDENTIAL

War Diary
of
151 Machine Gun Company.

From 1st to 31st March 1917.

Volume XIV

Army Form C. 2118.

Page 1.

WAR DIARY
or
INTELLIGENCE SUMMARY.
(Erase heading not required.)

Instructions regarding War Diaries and Intelligence Summaries are contained in F.S. Regs., Part II. and the Staff Manual respectively. Title pages will be prepared in manuscript.

Place	Date	Hour	Summary of Events and Information	Remarks and references to Appendices
In the Field	March 1st		In trenches facing FRESNES. Major Peckle of 175 M.G.C. arrived, in anticipation of relief. Two raids were made on enemy line. Our guns gave assistance, covering the flanks. The raid on Dragon Wood was successful, our prisoners being brought back. Fire was opened at moment the raiding parties were due to enter enemy trenches.	
	2nd			
	4th		Major Peckle left + Capt Benns of 174 Coy took his place, as the former Company was isolated with breakdown.	
	5th		4 Section Officers of 174 M.G.C. + 16 O.R.s arrived to be instructed in trench work.	
	6th			
	night of 7/8		Hay Coy (C + D Sections) was relieved by Nos 1 + 2 Sections of 174 M.G.C. The relieved Sections returned to billets (huts) at Joncourt.	
	night of 8/9		Remaining Half Company (A + B Sections + HQ) relieved, and proceeded to billets at Joncourt.	
	9th		The whole Company moved at 2.30 p.m. to billets (huts) Cant 5th Moncourt.	

Army Form C. 2118.

WAR DIARY
or
INTELLIGENCE SUMMARY.

(Erase heading not required.)

Page 2.

Place	Date	Hour	Summary of Events and Information	Remarks and references to Appendices
	March 10th		Cleaning up billets.	
	11.		(Sunday). Resting men & refitting.	
	12		Resting & refitting.	
	13th		In training at MORCOURT. See Appendices I. - Training Programme.
	To 29"			
	30"		Short Route March for Company, & cleaning up camp. All transport marched to ST GRATIEN.	
	31"		The Company entrained under Brigade arrangements at 9.30 am. detraining at TALMAS & proceeded to VIGOGNE. Transport marched from ST GRATIEN to VICOGNE.	

A M Morton Lieut.
O.C. 171 M.G.C.

Appendix 1(a)

151 M Gun Coy

Training Programme 1st Week

Time	13th Tuesday	14th Wednesday	15th Thursday	16th Friday	17th Saturday	18th Sunday
7.30 am to 8 am	Physical drill	do	do	do	do	Rest
9.30 am to 10.15 am	Morning Gun drill	do	do	do	do	—
10.30 to 11.15	ROUTE MARCH	Gun drill	Saturday gun exercises for Officers	Aiming drill	Nom. trigger press	—
11.30 to 12.15		A C to D Sect Inspection of small arms	A 2nd Sect Inspection of small arms	Rehearsal of guard mounting	Rehearsal afternoon guard mounting	—
12.30 to 1.15 pm	Feet inspection afterwards	Feet inspection afterwards	Mountable acts	Feet inspection acts	Feet inspection for fleas	—

Range Allotment
A B C & D Sects respectively

Wednesday. 10.30 am to 1.30 pm. application stopping
Thursday. do
Friday.   do
Saturday. do

A Bailey
12/3/17   OC 151 M Gun Coy

Appendix 1(B)

151st M. Gun Coy
Training Programme

2nd week - March 19th - 25th 1917

Time	Monday	Tuesday	Wednesday	Thursday	Friday	Saturday	Sunday
7.15 to 7.45 am	Physical Training	-- do --	-- do --	-- do --	-- do --	-- --	Rest
9 - 9.30 am	Gun Cleaning	-- do --	-- do --	-- do --	-- do --	-- do --	--
9.45 - 10.30 am	Gas drill with box respirators	Arms Drill	Saluting Drill	Gas drill with box respirators	Fire Orders	Squad Drill	--
10.45 - 11.30 am	Saluting & Arms Drill	{ Route March followers up	Guard mounting	Arms Drill	{ Company Drill followers up	{ Route march followers up by inspection of feet	--
11.45 am - 12.30 pm	Overhauling M.G.	{ Inspection of feet	Range (sure) Lecture (Stoppage)	Advanced Guard Drill	{ fields of fire (selection)		--
- 1.15 pm	Stoppages	-- do --	Selection of fire Indicator targets Recognition	-- do --	-- do --	--	--

Monday - A & B Sections (5 groups) Long range at Q.16
Wednesday - C Section (4 groups) -- do --
Thursday - D -- do --

N.W. Taylor
Lieut.
O.C. 151 M.G. Coy.

Appendix 1(c)

151st MACHINE GUN COY

TRAINING PROGRAMME
(MARCH 24th – 30th)

Time	24th Saturday	25 Sunday	26 Monday	27 Tuesday	28 Wednesday	29 Thursday	30 Friday
7:15 – 7:45	Physical Training	—	P	H	Y	S	I	C	A	L T	R	A	I	N	I	N	G
9 – 9:30	Gun Cleaning	—	G	U	N C	L	E	A	N	I	N	G
9:45 – 10:30	Squad Drill	10 to 12 Baths	Placing Guns for defence (Locally Q22 & 23)	Route marches	Communication & Ammunition	Gun Drill in box respirators
10:45 – 11:45	Route March			Following up Infantry	Supply in Attack	Rests Indirect Shoots
12 – 1:15	Followed by Indication of fire			Outskirting & clearing 13/15	Indirect Shoots Officers	Stoppages Judging Distance

Tuesday 27th }
Wednesday 28th } 12 – N.S.I. Fire 25 yards range 10 – 9.4
Thursday 29th } 27.P.12. for recently joined men.

27.P.12. Transport Route March (7 miles)

W Begley
Lieut
O.C 151th G.G.Coy

WAR DIARY
or
INTELLIGENCE SUMMARY.

Army Form C. 2118.

WAR DIARY
OF
151 MACHINE GUN COMPANY.
FROM 1ST TO 30TH APRIL 1917.

(CONFIDENTIAL)

VOLUME No. IX

Army Form C. 2118.

WAR DIARY
or
INTELLIGENCE SUMMARY.
(Erase heading not required.)

Page '

Instructions regarding War Diaries and Intelligence Summaries are contained in F. S. Regs., Part II. and the Staff Manual respectively. Title pages will be prepared in manuscript.

Place	Date	Hour	Summary of Events and Information	Remarks and references to Appendices
LA VICOGNE	1/4/17.		Sunday.	
GEZAINCOURT	2/4/17		Marched here.	
LIGNY-SUR CANCHE	3/4/17		" "	
CRISELLES	4/4/17		" "	
	5th + 6th		Stayed "	
FOSSEUX	7/4/17		Marched here.	
RICAMETZ	8/4/17		" "	
AMBRINES				
	9/4/17		Halted.	
AGNEZ-lès-DUISANS	10.4.17		Marched here weather bad.	
RONVILLE CAVES	11.4.17		" " arriving on 12th remainder of Night coln. Capt RASTON arrived
RONVILLE	12.4.17		to Billets here. 2 sections sent up the line 2 sections despatched later.
			Coy HQ east of Telegraph Hill
	13.4.17		Remainder of Coy arrive Coy HQ. 2 sections at Coy HQ move up
			to place 2 section opposite WANCOURT who take part in the
	14.4.17		fight on WANCOURT ridge. 1 section is given forward in support
			D section loses 3 guns and C section has one hit 22 casualties

R.W. Parker Lt 157th Coy
30.4.17

WAR DIARY
or
INTELLIGENCE SUMMARY.
(Erase heading not required.)

Army Form C. 2118.

Page 2

Place	Date	Hour	Summary of Events and Information	Remarks and references to Appendices
RONVILLE	14/4/17		Coy returns to billets	
	15/22/4/17		rpts Capt RALSTON goes to hospital on 16/4/17	
WANCOURT	22/4/17		Coy again takes the field opposite WANCOURT, 2 sections fire during	
	23/4/17		Artillery barrage. And push on afterwards	
" Town ridge	24/4/17		Order 12 guns can be manned	
	25/4/17		Relieved by 42 MG Coy – Casualties during this spell in trenches 27 including 2nd Lt H Lewis & 2nd Lt R L Hill	
RONVILLE	26/4/17		In Billets	
ARRAS	27/4/17		Total Marched to, left by train 9 pm for WARLINCOURT HALTE	
HUMBERCOURT	27/4/17		Arrived	
	28/30/4/17		In rest	

RPS orders
DL 157 McL on
30.4.17

Army Form C. 2118.

WAR DIARY
or
INTELLIGENCE SUMMARY.
(Erase heading not required.)

APPENDIX I

Place	Date	Hour	Summary of Events and Information	Remarks and references to Appendices
In the Field.	3/4/17		JOINED	
			Lieut. L. C. Tomlinson from 9th D.L.I. Auth. AG.	
	11th		Captain. D. Ralston. (as O.C.) from MGC Base Depot.	
	15th		2nd Lieut. H.T. Madock. do	
	22.		2nd Lieut. T.S. Macklin. do	
			QUITTED	
	18th		Captain. Ralston. D. Sick to Hospital.	
	24.		2nd Lieut. Hill. R.C. wounded in action.	
	25		" Lewis. H. do	
			Casualties - ORs	
	14th		ORs Killed in action.- 1. ORs wounded in action. 15. ORs wounded and missing. 1	
	23"		" " 1. " " 2 ORs	
	24"		" " 3 " " 7 ORs	
			Reinforcements received from M/Gun Corps Base Depot.	
	1st		ORs 7.	
	22.		" 12.	
	28.		" 21.	

Vol 12

WAR DIARY.

151st MACHINE GUN COMPANY.

MAY. 1917.

VOLUME. 16.

Army Form C. 2118.

WAR DIARY
or
INTELLIGENCE SUMMARY.
(Erase heading not required.)

WAR DIARY.

151st MACHINE GUN COMPANY

VOLUME XVI

MAY 1st TO 31st 1917

Army Form C. 2118.

WAR DIARY
or
INTELLIGENCE SUMMARY.
(Erase heading not required.)

151 M.G. Coy.

Place	Date	Hour	Summary of Events and Information	Remarks and references to Appendices
HUMBERCOURT	1.5.17		Preparations to move forward from park dumped.	
POMMIER	2.5.17		(First Lt) men report for duty. 2.40 pm starts for POMMIER. 4.15 pm move to BAILLEUVAL arrive at 6 pm. Capt D RALSTON takes over command from Lt. R. Bailey.	
BAILLEUVAL	3.5.17		Billets at BAILLEUVAL awaiting orders.	
	4.5.17		Move back to HUMBERCOURT. Coy Strength 10 Officers 151 men 7 hospital	
HUMBERCOURT	5.5.17		9.30 Staff ride 4 pm C. section to SAVVY for anti aircraft. 2nd Lt Gardner arrives. Amusement in evening	
	6.5.17		day on range + overhead fire stoppages (selection of positions)	
	7.5.17		hot day. Mechanism etc in billets. Guns fitted with deviced muzzle cap + bones.	
	8.5.17		Attack scheme along with 9th D.L.I. Ball ammunition was used by section	
	9.5.17		firing overhead both to practise sections + gun completions to infantry. Scheme entirely successful. Officers in the field.	
	10.5.17		Similar scheme with 8 DLI	
	11.5.17		Practise on range. A.M. section gun drills etc near billets. 7th O.R. reinforcements report from Div. depot Baillieul.	
	12.5.17		Similar scheme to 9/5/17. with 5 Borders. Col Lockett XVIII Corps MGO present	

Army Form C. 2118.

WAR DIARY
or
INTELLIGENCE SUMMARY.
(Erase heading not required.)

151 M.G. Coy

Place	Date	Hour	Summary of Events and Information	Remarks and references to Appendices
HUMBERCOURT	13.5.17		Sunday. Batt. C.O.s visited with view to cooperation in field firing schemes. 2nd Lt R Gardner to Hospital. A/Burn relieved C Section at SAULTY.	
	14.5.17		Wet day. Afternoon limber drill.	
	15.5.17		Devoured field firing scheme. New C.S.M. Millar arrived, 33 O.R. transferred to 150 M/Coy. 12 O.R. b/u 9 Coy.	
	16.5.17		Bath in billets. Coy passed thro gas chamber. Sgt Murrough, Pte Moreen, Pte Hardy, 1st Hetherington awarded Military Medal.	
	17.5.17		Wet day. 3 ammn. billets. Length taken through scheme for defence of HUMBERCOURT. XV ann relieve section en route at SAULTY then return to HUMBERCOURT.	
MONCHY AU BOIS	18.5.17		Left HUMBERCOURT 7.45 A.M. & marched to MONCHY AU-BOIS. 1 p.m. Coy bivouacked. Coy Strength 175 O.R. 2nd Lt Dutton to H.Q. School course.	
	19.5.17		Cleans guns, ammun. filled belts, leave opened.	
	20.5.17		Inspection of transport by B.G.C.	
	21.5.17		7.30 Stunt tramway put part in Bde Scheme S.oy RAMSART returning to billets from 7.30 pm took part in Night scheme. Sgt Hodkin awarded bar to Military Medal.	
	22.5.17		Wet.	

Army Form C. 2118.

WAR DIARY
or
INTELLIGENCE SUMMARY.
(Erase heading not required.)

151 M.G. Coy

Place	Date	Hour	Summary of Events and Information	Remarks and references to Appendices
MONCHY -au- BOIS	23/5/17		3.20 A.M. orders to move. Started 8.30 A.M. marched to SAULTY. arrived 11.30 A.M.	
SAULTY	24.5.17		Inspections. 2nd LT T.S BLACKTIN to hospital. 4.pm march to SOUASTRE.	
SOUASTRE	25.5.17		Coy strength 167 O.R. Tommy-gun front course.	
	26.5.17		Gun drill + bath. 65 men inoculated. LT R.L Bailey awarded M.C.	
	27.5.17		Church parade	
	28.5.17		Training - range practice, etc.	
	29.5.17		Route march - practice with German gun. 2nd Lt T.G.R Trowbridge to hospital	
	30.5.17		Range fatigue - intensive digging	
	31.5.17		One of gunners wounded - Baillon.	

J Ralston Cyster
OC 151 M.G Coy

Army Form C. 2118.

WAR DIARY
or
INTELLIGENCE SUMMARY.
(Erase heading not required.)

Vol 13

WAR DIARY.
151ST MACHINE GUN COMPANY.
JUNE 1917.
VOLUME 17.

Army Form C. 2118.

WAR DIARY
or
INTELLIGENCE SUMMARY.
(Erase heading not required.)

WAR DIARY
OF
151st MACHINE GUN COMPANY

JUNE 1ST - 30TH 1917

VOLUME XVII

WAR DIARY
or
INTELLIGENCE SUMMARY

Army Form C. 2118.

151 Infantry Brigade

Place	Date	Hour	Summary of Events and Information	Remarks and references to Appendices
SOUASTRE	1/6/17		Men in huts & officers billeted in village. Training as Appendix I	Training Appendix I
	2/6/17		O.C. Coy & officers & N.C.Os visit old fighting grounds of the Somme - from HIGH WOOD to BUTTE de WARLINCOURT	
	3/6/17		Sunday - Church Parade	
	4/6/17		Training - Lt Shrubsoly reports from Division.	
	5/6/17		In place of Training Programme - Brigade Scheme - Attack & defence of Bonquivillers - in Ceremonial parade & march past followed conclusion of field operations. Coys were engaged from 5am to 4pm. No man fell out though interval of hot	
	6/6/17		Only two hours parade (request of B.G.C.)	
	7/6/17		Training - fighting strength 10 offrs. 172 O.R.	
	8/6/17		do	
	9/6/17		do - Lt Butler returned from M.G. Course.	
	10/6/17		Sunday - Church Parade - Lt Graham proceeds on leave U.K. - M.O. inspected Kitchens.	
	11/6/17		Training - weather bad.	
	12/6/17		Modified training. Kermis (repetition of Coy sports & See - beat Transport Lines Training (Range practice) - O.C. reconnoitred 53rd Inf Coy Sector (CHERISY).	
	13/6/17		Preparations for going into line - Zt Jones reports from course (infantry) fighting strength - 9 offrs. 182 O.R.	
	14/6/17			
N. MERCATEL	15/6/17		Left SOUASTRE at 7.30 am for appropriates (M36 & 9.4) near MERCATEL to take over from 53rd Coy of the A.T.N. Division (114) - A Half car in relay to H.Q. NZER for W Llinvis - Lt 30 pm march resumed. Coy arrived at (Inty) at 7pm	

E.R. Baker Capt.

Army Form C. 2118.

151 M.G. Coy

WAR DIARY
or
INTELLIGENCE SUMMARY.
(Erase heading not required.)

Instructions regarding War Diaries and Intelligence Summaries are contained in F.S. Regs., Part II. and the Staff Manual respectively. Title pages will be prepared in manuscript.

Place	Date	Hour	Summary of Events and Information	Remarks and references to Appendices
N: MERCATEL	16-6-17		2.30 pm teams left camp at ½ hour intervals to relieve 53rd Coy in the line facing CHERISY. Front line D Section (3 teams) – Support C Section (3 teams) – Reserve – A Section 4 teams – at MERCATEL B Section 4 teams at H.Q.-C. Harassing fire nightly by front line and teams (this is daily programme) Reconnaissance of ground with view to adequately meeting the tactical situation (Coy in line)	
N: HENINEL	17-6-17			
	18-6-17		H.Q.Coy moved to N.22.d.9.2 leaving transport & personnel at MERCATEL camp. Scheme based on Reconnaissance made on 17th instituted & Coy in the line.	
	19-6-17		Intersection relief – B relieving D, D.C, C–A, A back to Transport lines. 2 O.R. wounded front line system	
	20-6-17		Coy in line – early morning 1 O.R. killed from leave – (Coy strength 9 Offrs – 183 O.R.) Lt Graham returns from leave – Larger programme of endeavour fire arranged to be continued daily, & enemy tracks & further endeavour fire positions constructed. (Coy in line)	
	23-6-17		Bde (less 151 MG Coy) relieved by 149 Inf.Bn.	
	24-6-17		Intersection relief in Coy – position being A Section in front system & guns in further gun being introduced – B Section in support – D Section (2 guns) reserve, C Section 4 guns (reserve) 3 guns resting at Transport.	
	25-6-17		2Lt Thirtle-Hay wounded on front line – he remains at duty. 6 OR. casualties. Lt Morton reported as joining the Coy. 2Lt Perelin leaves to England.	
	26-6-17		(Coy in line)	
	27-6-17		"	
	28-6-17		Intersection relief – C Section under (Lt Motte) front system – A (less – 1 gun) in support – B system in reserve. A Section 10 guns 180 O.R. – Area held by 167 Coy. Coy strength reconnoitred.	

W. Roberton-Bagshott
Capt

A.S.834 Wt. W4973/M687 750,000 8/16 D. D. & L. Ltd. Forms/C.2118/13.

WAR DIARY
or
INTELLIGENCE SUMMARY.

(Erase heading not required.)

Army Form C. 2118.

151 In[f]y Coy

Place	Date	Hour	Summary of Events and Information	Remarks and references to Appendices
Nr HENINEL	29/4/17		Area held by 151 Coy reconnoitred. Conference by 149 Inf Coy forwarded to Camp at M 36 b 9-4 near MERCATEL	
Nr MERCATEL	30/4/17		Relief completed at 1 to 10 am 30th Coy resting + cleaning up — very wet day.	

D Wilkin Capt

Map 57D.

Training Programme   11/6/17 – 16/6/17

Date	Locality	Training
11/6/17	D 16 d 5.3	Range finding, judging distances, map reading.
	D 23 a	Digging in guns.
12/6/17	D 23 a & b	Mounting gun in lowest position & with light Tripod
	D 14 c	Use of ground & cover
13/6/17	Bayencourt, Coigneux	Route march with Limbers.
	Camp	Insp" of Gas appliances & Gas drill
14/6/17	E 23 c	Indication & recognition
	Transport lines	Limber packing & cleaning
15/6/17	Between Souastre & Fonquevillers	Ammunition supply – use of mules.
	Camp	Insp" of Kit by section officers
16/6/17	Transport lines	German Gun
	do	mechanism, cleaning guns etc.

Map 57D.

Training Programme   APPENDIX I.
    28/5/17 – 2/6/17

Date	Locality	Training
28/5/17	D 16 d 5-3	Range finding, & judging distances Mechanism, Stoppages, Map reading.
	D 23 d	Indirect fire.
29/5/17	HENU – ST AMAND	Route march
	D 27 b.	German Gun.
30/5/17	BRIGADE SCHEME	
31/5/17	D 23 a	Use of ground & cover. Digging in Guns.
1/6/17	E 26 a 5-2	Indirect Barrage fire
	D 22 b 1-6	Cleaning Guns.
2/6/17	AS ON 31st MAY.	

Mat
57p

Training Programme 4/6/17 - 9/6/17

Date	Locality	Training
4/6/17	K 3 b 2.5 Transport Lines	Indication & recognition of targets. Mechanism
5/6/17	St Amand, Pommers, Bienvillers	Route march. Judging distance.
6/6/17	D 23 a & b. D 24 c	Mounting gun in lowest position & with light tripod Use of Ground & cover
7/6/17	Range 'A'	Firing
8/6/17	E 23 c Transport field	Indication & recognition Mechanism
9/6/17	D 23 a & b	Digging Gun positions (strong points) Judging distance

WAR DIARY. Vol 14

151st Machine Gun Coy

JULY 1917

VOLUME No XVIII

151

Army Form C. 2118.

WAR DIARY
or
INTELLIGENCE SUMMARY.
(Erase heading not required.)

WAR DIARY
of
151ST MACHINE GUN COMPANY
From July 1st, 1917.
to August 31st, 1917

VOLUME XVIII

R. Austin Capt.
Comdg 151st M.G. Coy.

Army Form C. 2118.

WAR DIARY
or
INTELLIGENCE SUMMARY.

(Erase heading not required.)

151st M. Gun Coy.

Instructions regarding War Diaries and Intelligence Summaries are contained in F. S. Regs., Part II. and the Staff Manual respectively. Title pages will be prepared in manuscript.

Place	Date	Hour	Summary of Events and Information	Remarks and references to Appendices
MERCATEL	1/7/17		Map 51-B-S.W. In reserve area - Reconnaissance of line by C.O. (Cavalry Farm WANCOURT Tower) Left sector held by 168 M.G.Coy. - Right sector by 167 M.G. (COJeuldge)	
	2nd		C.& D. sections relieved 167 Coy. (right sector) in line - C. section in tool system. O.C. proceeded with these sections soon after relief, enemy shelled heavily & is supposed to have attempted an attack.	
N.16 a. 1.7.	3rd		A & B sections + H.Q. proceeded up line & relieved 168 Coy. (Major Roberts) in left sector - Relief complete 1 am 4 inst. H.Q. - N16.a.1.7. Transport lines & camp retained at M.35 & 9.4 near MERCATEL.	
	4th		Scheme prepared & submitted to Brigade for defence of whole Brigade front by Barrage - Scheme approved.	
	5th		Cos in line. Harassing fire on selected spots - (expenditure 9 guns 179 O.R.) (C. & D)	
	6th		do Interdiction relief do (A & B)	
	7th		do Considerable enemy aircraft activity.	
	8th		Lt A.M. Jones M.C. & Lt Sheryngs reported for duty. Harassing fire programme carried out & continued through period in trenches.	
	9th		Brigadier in General inspected gun positions Trenches - work & worrying Boche continued - & along with C.O. North of Cojeul R.	
	10th		Preparation made to assist (with 4 guns by indirect fire) 12th Div on left in an attack - Guns on North slope of WANCOURT Ridge. One OR killed - one wounded. Enemy aircraft active.	

Army Form C. 2118.

WAR DIARY
or
INTELLIGENCE SUMMARY.

(Erase heading not required.)

151st M Gun Coy.

Place	Date 1917	Hour	Summary of Events and Information	Remarks and references to Appendices
N 16 a 1.7.	July 11th		Boche anticipated attack taking a trench at 5am - our attack for 7.30 am "still on". Interaction relief (C+D). Lt G. Morton wounded (slightly). (on strength 11 Offrs, 176 o.R.	
	12th		OC accompanied DW M.G.O. round whole sector with reference to Div. by Gun defence scheme. Interaction relief (A + B). Lt Furlongs in charge of B Section Lt furlongs - work carried out in reference to new Div. scheme of defence.	
	13th		Lt Inches - work carried out in reference to new Div. scheme of defence. Aerial activity marked.	
	14th		Preparation made with 6 guns to assist attack by 12 Div. to regain Longtrench. 2 Lt J.R. Graham proceeds to Tancport Lines.	
	15th		Opened barrage fire at 5am in conjunction with artillery to assist 12 D.W (on left) - Aerial activity marked. Heavy rain - Division did not attack.	
	16th		A section of 149 M.G. Coy under Lt Fletcher attached to this Coy for purpose of barrage fire 5 + 6 and 12 Div. to recover Long Trench.	
	17th	4.45 am	Barrage opened - attack only partially successful - further barrage arranged for evening.	
		9.45 pm	Attack successful. A message of neighbourly thanks received from 37th M.G. Coy - about 35,000 rounds fired. LT Boulton to Hospital sick.	
	18th		Orders received to hand over guns in accordance with Div. scheme to 149 Coy (on right sector). C + D Sections relieved by two sections of 149 Coy. Two guns of C section retained in Trenches for the night to assist 12 Div. if necessary by barrage fire. Guns on right sector altered to new diamond positions.	

WAR DIARY
or
INTELLIGENCE SUMMARY. 151 M/Gun Coy.

(Erase heading not required.)

Army Form C. 2118.

Place	Date 1917 July	Hour	Summary of Events and Information	Remarks and references to Appendices
MERCATEL	19th		Left sector relieved by 149 M.G. Coy. - whole Coy back at Camp near MERCATEL - (Coy strength 11 officers 175 O.R.	
	20th		Resting — Lt Morton from Hospital (light duty). At midnight 19/20th (OC name J/Coy changed from "FISCAL" to "BUFF."	
	21st		Resting cleaning Lt I.A Lauder & 7 O.R. reinforcements reported	
	22nd		do Guns overhauled by Ordnance	
	23rd		do Inspection by O.C.	
	24th		Three guns of A Sec'n to support line to succour 150 M.G. Coy.	
	25th		Preparations for returning to line	
	26th		C and D sections & remaining gun of A Section - relieved sections of 150 Coy in the line. O.C. moved up with them. (Coy strength 12 Off 181 O.R.) Coy HQ - N.22.a.9.2	
	27th		B Section moved up to Reserve positions. O.C. made reconnaissance of line as handed over by outgoing Company.	
	28th		B section in reserve position relieved A Section in line. The fine opportunity for using the new tracer bullets was exceedingly successful. Harassing fire carried out each night on enemy tracks, road, dumps etc.	
	29th		Guns put out of action by Trench Mortar fire in Dead Boche Sap.	

Army Form C. 2118.

WAR DIARY
or
INTELLIGENCE SUMMARY.   151 M/Gun Coy
(Erase heading not required.)

Place	Date	Hour	Summary of Events and Information	Remarks and references to Appendices
N22 d 9-2	1917 July 30		Intersection relief during afternoon & evening.	
	31		Gun put out of action & Tripod absolutely destroyed by German mortar fire.	

B. Bolton. Capt.
O.C. Mag 151 M/gun Coy

Vol 15

WAR DIARY.

151st Machine Gun Company.

August, 1917.

VOLUME — XIX.

WAR DIARY or INTELLIGENCE SUMMARY

(Erase heading not required.)

151st M.G. Coy

August 1917

Army Form C. 2118.

Place	Date 1917	Hour	Summary of Events and Information	Remarks and references to Appendices
HENINEL	Aug. 1		Company in line facing CHERISY (8 guns in front system - 4 in support - 4 in reserve) Harassing fire nightly.	
	2.		Ground reviewed by C.O. with a view to selecting better positions for guns in saps. (Coy. strength 12 officers 180 O.R.).	
	3.		Intensive relief.	
	4.		C.O. + Brigadier General examined line in view of relief of support guns by 1 Div. M.G. Coy (245 Coy). Reinforcements received - 1, 2 O.R.	
	5.		Three guns C Section in front system relieved by 150 M.G. Coy in consequence of a side-slip to the right. Reinforcements received - 5 O.R.	
	6.		Three guns (support) relieved by 245 Coy (Div. M.G. Coy). C Section to transport (camp near Mercatel). B Section relieved Section of 62 M.G. Coy on right in consequence of side slip movement. Reinforcements - 1 O.R.	
	7.		2/Lt Maddocks assisted Brigadier Genl. to select positions for covering fire for proposed scheme. O.C. + D.M.G.O. inspected line. Transfers :- 1 O.R. to 62 M.G. Coy ; 1 O.R. to 245 M.G. Coy ; 2 O.R. to 49th M.G. Coy	
	8.		Raid by 5th Border Regt - enemy trench found empty - (covering fire afforded.)	
	9.		13 hour bombardment on left. 12th Div on left made a successful raid in evening. C Section relieved A Section who went to camp near Mercatel. (Coy strength 12 officers 195 O.R.)	

Army Form C. 2118.

WAR DIARY
or
INTELLIGENCE SUMMARY.

(Erase heading not required.)

August 1917.
151 M.G. Coy.

Place	Date 1917	Hour	Summary of Events and Information	Remarks and references to Appendices
HENINEL	Aug. 10		In the line. H.Q. N.22.d.9.2. (map 51B S.W.)	
	11.		Raid by 6 D.L.I. - Covering fire provided by this Company.	
	12.		Relieved by 149 M.G Coy during daylight. Company proceeded to (camp near MERCATEL. Training programme submitted.	Training programme attached.
Near MERCATEL	13.		Company in Camp - Cleaning Guns, equipment etc.	
	14.		— do — (Cleaning generally, inspection for repairing purposes. Improvements to bivouacs.	
	15.		Training - range practices. Percentage of men on days leave to AMIENS	
	16.		— do — Inspection - Physical training expert much appreciated. (Coy strength 12 officers 191 O.R.)	
	17.		— do — Range practices. O.C. (Capt. Ralston on leave to U.K. Lt Bailey M.C. in charge.	
	18.		— do — Horse Show VI Corps - O.C. inspects line preparatory to taking over. Meets O.C. 245 M.G.Coy. & arranges relief of one gun on relief by 150 M.G.Coy. Camp for Reserve Section selected on Sunken Road S.E. of NEUVILLE VITASSE.	
	19.		10 guns relieved 150 M.G. Coy (9 guns) & 245 M.G. Coy (1 gun) - O.C. stayed at 150 M.G. H.Q. Line of WANCOURT TOWER ridge.	

Army Form C. 2118.

WAR DIARY
or
INTELLIGENCE SUMMARY.
(Erase heading not required.)

Instructions regarding War Diaries and Intelligence Summaries are contained in F. S. Regs., Part II. and the Staff Manual respectively. Title pages will be prepared in manuscript.

Place	Date 1917	Hour	Summary of Events and Information	Remarks and references to Appendices
WANCOURT - FEUCHY LINE	Aug. 20		A Section completed move into new Reserve (camp near NEUVILLE VITASSE. Relief of 2 g 150 M.G. Coy guns (completed in Left Sector. H.Q. at N16.b.1.8. WANCOURT FEUCHY Line (Map 51.B.SW)	
	21.		In the line. Harassing fire nightly.	
	22.		— do — 1 O.R. wounded.	
	23.		Interaction Relief. A Section relieved C; C – D; D to camp. (Coy strength 12 officers 190 O.R.)	
	24.		In the line. Quiet except for M.G's at night.	
	25.		Lot of work at new positions	
	26.			
	27.		Relief of sections postponed owing to proposed scheme. Scheme off owing to very heavy rain	
	28.		Partial interaction relief. D relieved A; A – B; B to camp. Very quiet bright night.	
	29.		Quiet in line - weather stormy	
	30.		— do — except for M.G. fire. Capt Ralston returned from leave	
	31.		— do — Relief (Interaction) – B sec relieves D; D – C; C to camp. Harassing fire. Gas projected from our line	

R.W Morley Lt Capt
Cmdg 157 M.G. Coy.

Copy. 151st M. G. Coy.

TRAINING PROGRAMME.

August 13th. to 19th. 1917.

DATE.	TIME.	UNIT.	PLACE.	NATURE of TRAINING.	REMARKS.
13th	9 A.M. to 1 P.M. + 2 P.M. to 3 P.M.	151st. M.Gun Coy.	Camp.	Overhauling Guns & Gun Kit. Inspection of Gas Respirators.	General Clean-up.
14th	9 A.M. to 1 P.M. + 2 P.M. to 3.30 P.M.	do	do	Squad Drill. Saluting. Clean -ing S.A.A. in Belts. Inspection by Bdn. Officer.	Between in Highting order went out Gases.
15th	9 A.M. to 1 P.M.	do	Range at M.23.6.7.7.	Firing Practice.	—
16th	9 A.M. to 1 P.M.	do	Camp.	Transport and Company Inspection. Gas Drill.	Games in Afternoon.
17th	9 A.M. to 1 P.M.	do	Range at M.19.A (central)	Firing Exercises.	—
18th	9 A.M. to 1 P.M.	do	Camp.	Physical Exercise. Gun Drill. Squad Drill.	Games in Afternoon.
19th	9 A.M. to 1 P.M.	do	do	Squad Drill. Route March.	— do —

13/8/1917.

(Sgd.) D. Ralston. Capt.
Comdg. 151st M. G. Coy.

N.16.6.1.8.

WAR DIARY. 9/16

151st Machine Gun Company.

September 1917.

Volume — XX

WAR DIARY or INTELLIGENCE SUMMARY

Army Form C. 2118.

Place	Date	Hour	Summary of Events and Information	Remarks and references to Appendices
COJEUL VALLEY SECTOR.	1/9/17		Coy. 5/B. S.W.B. 1 Offr. 11 O.R's as reinforcements.	
N.16.B.18. Coy. H.A.	2/9/17		Coy. in Line. 11 O.R's as reinforcements. Successful Raid by 12th Division. Coy assist by 1 Gun, this in daylight. At night, Coy. caused with covering fire the withdrawal of Stokes Gunners and 8th D.L.I. who from forward position in No-Man's Land staged S.T. ROMART QUARRY. Coil Valley. 5 guns employed 2 at S Coy. ex-operating Stokes and infantry support thereon at the way hostile M.G's. were silenced amongst retirement.	
	3/9/17		In the trenches.	
CARLISLE LINES BEAURAINS	4/9/17		Anti Aircraft Gun mounted at N.H. Relieved by the 149th M.G. Coy. Coy. to the Carlisle Lines, near Beaurains.	
M.16.d.9.1.	5/9/17		Clean up. Inspection & Kit Rect.	
	6/9/17		Two Guns on Anti-aircraft duty in Brigade area. Coy. Strength 11 Offrs + 251 x. Training when possible. 4 Offrs on Working Parties.	
	7/9/17		" " " " " " " " " " "	
	8/9/17		" " " " " " " " " " "	
	9/9/17		" " " " " " " " " " "	
	10/9/17		" " " " " " " " " " "	
	11/9/17		"D" Section to line for emplacements digging for start on the 15th inst.	
	12/9/17		Working Parties from other Sections supplied line. 100,000 Rounds in Millesboxes sent to Position.	

WAR DIARY
or
INTELLIGENCE SUMMARY.

(Erase heading not required.)

Army Form C. 2118.

Place	Date	Hour	Summary of Events and Information	Remarks and references to Appendices
CHERISY SECTOR. COY H.Q. at M.16.B.9.1.	13/9/17		Coy. relieved the 150th M.G. Coy. in their Barry Coy. H.Q. on the Quarry in FOSTER AVENUE. 300Y rds B.9.9. linked to outpost positions. Work on these positions.	
	14/9/17		In trenches. Work on Coy's positions.	
	15/9/17	4.0 P.M	In trenches – RAID by the 1st D.L.I. at 4.0 P.M. 13 officer and 150th M.G Coy. and assistance from the Vickers [?] guns of over 20 prisoners made. The enemy shewn enthusiasm [?]	
		4.40 P.M	Smaller raid on northern portion of our Barry front on first Red Road Trench. 2 Vickers machine [?] guns in barrage.	
	16/9/17	1.30 A.M	Gas Projection One group of Livens projectors [?] developed trouble in front line [?] and oil on them [?]	
			Coy. B. out. C. in. Sector Relief. "C" Section to the Reserve Camp. Right [?]	
			In trenches. Harassing fire. Coy. Strength 11 officers and 228 O.R.	
	17/9/17	"		
	18/9/17	"		
	19/9/17	"		
	20/9/17	"		
	21/9/17		Sector Relief. "A" Section to Reserve Camp. 3 officers attached for [?]	

WAR DIARY or INTELLIGENCE SUMMARY

Army Form C. 2118.

(Erase heading not required.)

Place	Date	Hour	Summary of Events and Information	Remarks and references to Appendices
CHERISY SECTOR and	22/9/17	—	12th Division Raid. Capt. Walden takes over the duties of the D.M.G.O. 2. R.L? Bailey in command. Harassing fire continued.	
	23/9/17		In trenches. Harassing M.G. fire.	
	24/9/17		"	
	25/9/17		Arrangements for Gas, Artillery and M.G. barrage in of our M.G's, taking parts Harassing fire.	
	26/9/17		Coo th. stripe put off. "A" section relieves "D" section and set action to Reserve camp. Coy. Strength 11 Offrs + 199 O.R.s. One Offr returned at Coy HQrs Harassing fire.	
	27/9/17 4.43 a.m.		Two Pls staff Guns fire in a.m. 3rd Divn. Sub-section of D to th Reserve camp. all men attached to Battalions returned in order there to be Coy. Unual harassing fire.	
	(idem) (after)		Small and resulting in 1 prisoner & about complete on German fire line first on enemy in rear of August Road, after Maldo had returned. Enemy also left 3 Guns had opened on NARROW TRENCH and CHERISY on the left of my morning. Above Trench Mortar Shoot. Usual Harassing fire. Passes of gob.	
	28/9/17		Relieved by the 149 x M.G. Coy. 2 casualties (O.R.) on day in trenches.	
	29/9/17		Returned to CARLISLE LINES. Lincoln BARRACKS. Both prisoners. Staff were M.G. fire at night on enemy Covalier, sweeping low over his	
CARLISLE LINES	30/9/17		In Huts. Returned to P Returned refit.	
N BEAURAINS				

Report on the Part taken by the 151st M.G. Coy. in operations of the 15/16th September, 1916, in Front of
CHERISY.

Map Ref.
513. S.W.
1/20,000

(1) TACTICAL.

Group "A". Consisting of six guns situated at T.6.A.7.6. in an old disused Trench running S.E. This Trench had gently rising ground to its front (N.E.), which effectively screened any observation from that direction, but had enfilade observation from the S.E., which was overcome by camouflage. Rising ground to the rear allowed of very accurate alignment of posts for direction.

Guns were placed 10 to 15 yards apart and was controlled by one Officer.

The Target for this Group was an Oblong Area including part of CHERRY WOOD, and suspected HQ.

The depth of the Target was searched by laying Guns in Pairs at a different range for each pair. Lateral searching was done by traversing inwards.

One Belt filling station in a deep dug-out about 25 yards distant supplied this Group. (Belt filling being done by both Hand and Machine).

Group "C". Consisting of four Guns situated in Cuckoo Reserve about 0.25.c.15/10, their line of fire being on a Magnetic Bearing of between 74° and 76°.

In this case the Guns were again laid in Pairs at different range and Magnetic Bearing for each Pair.

The Target was about 350 yards of NUT TRENCH and a portion of NIGHT TR, the centre of the Target being where NUT TR. joins NIGHT TR.

The fire was oblique and the Guns traversed 1° either way.

Belt supply - same as in "A" Group.

This position was only under observation from a long distance and could not see its Target.

One Officer controlled this Group.

Group "D". Consisting of three Guns situated in MALLARD TR. about 0.25.c.6.6.

The Target for this Group was 250 yards of NUT TR. from 0.21.c.10.25. to 0.21.c.36.

All these three Guns, were laid at different elevations and Magnetic Bearings.

REPORT (TACTICAL) contd. - 2

Group "D" contd:-

The line of fire was oblique, and the Guns traversed 1° either way.

One Officer controlled this Group.

Guns were not under Observation.

Belt supply the same as in other Groups.

(2) TECHNICAL.

All Guns fired well, except one which had a broken fusee spring, and trouble with its Feed Block. This Gun was from "D" Group.

Another Gun of "A" Group having fired very well in the first two phases did not fire in the third Phase, owing to the recoiling portions sticking - report not yet to hand from the Armourer re this Gun.

Where the enemy barrage was expected the emplacements were covered with a light shrapnel proof cover which proved very useful and undoubtedly saved casualities both to Guns and Personnel.

One Section experimented with Condensers, the most satisfactory being a framework of wood covered with expanded metal. This was let into the Parapet and covered up with earth except one blank end with a small hole in it for the Condenser Tube.

Night firing boxes were also experimented with and found satisfactory. These were made out of 18 pdr. empty cartridge cases. Sketches of this and also of the Condenser are being prepared, and will be submitted later.

An improvement in the depression stop in use was made by drilling a small hole through the coned end of the elevating joint pin, and inserting inserting a split pin so as to keep the Collar of the adjusting Rod from slipping off. We found out that the adjusting Nuts altered with the vibration of the Gun. This could be remedied by the use of jam-nuts.

A further examination is being made with reference to the Wear to Barrels, and also as to any defective S.A.A.

The latter we had not a great deal of trouble with.

REPORT, contd: 3.

(3) RETALIATION.

"A" Group escaped attention from the enemy altogether.

"C" Group had only a little shrapnel over it, and was not inconvenienced at all.

"D" Group got a good deal of attention, which was disconcerting, but did no damage as no direct hits were obtained by the enemy.

Rounds fired and Stoppages.

Group	Gun	1st Phase	Stoppages	Water	2nd Phase	Stoppages	Water	3rd Phase	Total
"A"	1	5,000	none	3 Gallons	3250	Broken Lock Spring.	3 Gallons	1250	9,500
	2	5,250	2 Muzzle Cups cottered. 1 Disc Split. 1 Broken Firing Pin.	3	3750	Bent String Pin Roller Lever	3	Nil (gum)	9,000
	3	5,250	Nº 4's Roller Pin	3	2750	Broken Fuzee & Nº 4's	3	500	8,500
	4	5,000	Broken Nº 4	3	4,000	Nº 4's	3	1,000	10,000
	5	5,000	Nº 4's + 2 Rmd Bolt + 1 Sq. Case.	3	3,500	Nº 2 Stoppages	3	1,250	9,750
	6	5,500	Roller Split Pin broken. Weak Lock Spring	3	2,500	2 Cross Feeds	3	1,500	9,500
"C"	1	4,250	Stoppages of the Sout, i.e.- Broken Lock Spring Firing Pin. Connecting Rod Separated Case Nº 3	4	3,500	Included in these set out on 1st Phase	3	Nil	7,750
	2			4	3,250		3	do	6,750
	3			4	3,250		3	do	6,750
	4			4	2,000		3	do	4,450
"D"	1	3750	none	3	450 (with London)	—	3	—	4,500
	2	3750	Bent + broken Firing Pin	3	3000	none Surtby trouble	3 galls	Nil	6,750
	3	750	Broken Lock Spring Weak Lock Spring	3	100		—	do	850

06 5,550-76,774

WAR DIARY. Oct 17

151st Machine Gun Company.

October 1917.

Volume XXI

WAR DIARY
or
INTELLIGENCE SUMMARY.

(Erase heading not required.)

Army Form C. 2118.

Place	Date	Hour	Summary of Events and Information	Remarks and references to Appendices
CARLISLE LINES.	1st		Coy in Divisional Reserve. Capt RALSTON at Divisional H.Q. as acting D.M.G.O. Lieut R.L.BAILEY.M.C. in Command.	
NEAR BEAURAINS	2nd		Company engaged in clearing up & preparations for moving fwd.	
	3rd		Camp fatigues.	
	4th		Company marched to GOMIECOURT. Coy billeted in tents & Bivouacs.	
	5th		Company resting & clearing up. Lieut R.L.BAILEY.M.C. left Coy to take over command of the 94th M.G. Company. Lieut A.M.JONES.M.C. as O.C.	
GOMIECOURT.	6th		Capt D RALSTON returns from Divisional H.Q. & takes over Command. Lieut A.M.JONES.M.C. as 2nd in Command.	
	7th		Company engaged in Camp fatigues.	
	8th		Weather very wet & stormy	
	9th		Brigade practice for March past on 10th inst.	

DR

WAR DIARY
or
INTELLIGENCE SUMMARY.
(Erase heading not required.)

Army Form C. 2118.

Place	Date	Hour	Summary of Events and Information	Remarks and references to Appendices
GOMIECOURT	10th		Brigade field day practicing attack formation & system of advance adopted from their experience on Flanders. Criticised by Major Gen'l of Brigade past Lieut General J.A.L. HALDANE, commander of 6th Corp. - Farewell speech by Corp Commander.	
	11th		Warning Order to move early on following day receiving that cancelled later. Company ordered to Stand To" & await further orders.	
	12th		Company remain ready to move at short notice.	Envy
	13th		Ditto. Later end of day all Movement Orders cancelled. Company spent the whole day on Ranges. Dennis's Staken in the Jutot Own head & Indirect Fire practices. Inter-Section Competition also held in the afternoon - in getting quickly into "Action" & opening Fire.	
	14th		Sunday. Church Parades in morning & rest for remainder of day.	
	15th		Orders for Coy to move received. Parking of Limbers & general preparation carried out.	

PAGE N° 3.

WAR DIARY
or
INTELLIGENCE SUMMARY.

Army Form C. 2118.

Place	Date	Hour	Summary of Events and Information	Remarks and references to Appendices
GOMMECOURT and BAPAUME	16th		Camp fatigues during morning. At about 6pm Coy proceeded by Transport march to BAPAUME & entrained there at 9.15pm. All complete & then left	
near ZEEGERS CAPPELLE	17th		BAPAUME at 9.45pm. Coy detrained at ESQUELBEC station at 6.30am on following morning. Coy 'fell in' & marched off to Billets in ERINGHAM area. Coy billeted in various barns near ZEEGERS CAPPELLE.	
	18th		Resting, cleaning up & general Camp fatigues.	
	19th		Weather very rough.	
LEDRINGHAM	20th		Orders received at 4.30am for move. Coy marched to LEDRINGHAM. Billeted in barns. Warning Order received at 10.15pm. Operation Order received at 11.45pm.	
NEAR PROVEN	21st		Coy moved off at 8.30am & marched via WORMHOUDT, HERZEELE, HOUTKERQUE, to PROVEN. Coy halted & dinners was taken en route. Coy billeted in Barns & Tents about 1 mile from PROVEN. The march was long, took the Coy arrived fairly fit & no one fell out.	

PAGE N° 4

Army Form C. 2118.

WAR DIARY
or
INTELLIGENCE SUMMARY.
(Erase heading not required.)

Instructions regarding War Diaries and Intelligence Summaries are contained in F. S. Regs., Part II. and the Staff Manual respectively. Title pages will be prepared in manuscript.

Place	Date	Hour	Summary of Events and Information	Remarks and references to Appendices
NEAR PROVEN.	22nd		Operation Order for move on next day received about 6a. Coy moved off at 1.15pm & marched to SALEM. CAMP arriving about 2.30pm.	
SALEM CAMP.	23rd		Coy engaged in lectures work.	
	24th		General camp fatigues. C.O. & 2nd in command reconnoitered forward area's.	
	25th		Weather very rough & Coy remained in Billets. During Order & Operation Order for move received during night.	
DUBLIN CAMP.	26th		Coy marched off at 9.30am & marched to DUBLIN CAMP. at A.10 d.6.8. near ELVERDINGHE. Move completed by 3.30pm & reported to Division & Brigade H.Q's. Lieut LANDLES & 2nd Lieut MADDOCKS with 23 O.R's left the Company to join Divisional Depot Battalion. Rain practically the whole day. Company billeted in huts in Wood.	
	28th		Cleaning Guns Equipment & Linlen packing reserve ammunition & Linlen packing	

PAGE N° 5. Army Form C. 2118.

WAR DIARY
or
INTELLIGENCE SUMMARY.
(Erase heading not required.)

Place	Date	Hour	Summary of Events and Information	Remarks and references to Appendices
DUBLIN CAMP. (A.12.d.6.8.)	28th		C.O. reconnoitred forward area & Trenches, part of Coy engaged on working party at BOSINGHE.	
	29th		Practically whole of Coy employed on R.E. work at BOSINGHE. Enemy Aircraft very active especially during night.	
	30th		2nd Lieut. GRAHAM & BUTLIN reconnoitred forward area & Trenches. Coy employed on overhauling guns & reserve ammunition. Operator Order for move into Line on night of 1/2 Nov November 1917 received.	
	31st		Practice attack near Camp by Brigade. C Section only employed, remainder of Coy engaged in preparing to move into the Line. 2nd in Command, Transport Officer, & Company Sergt Major visited present Coy in Line & reconnoitred gun positions &c. Coy strength 10 Officers & 186 O.R's.	

C.M.D.Q. [signature] Capt.
151. M.G. Coy.

WAR DIARY

151st Machine Gun Company

November, 1917

Volume — XXII

Army Form C. 2118.

WAR DIARY
or
INTELLIGENCE SUMMARY.
(Erase heading not required.)

151st M.G. Coy.

Place	Date	Hour	Summary of Events and Information	Remarks and references to Appendices
U18 c 5.6 (Sheet 20)	Nov 1917 1st		NOVEMBER 1917 Company Strength 10 offr - 187 O.R. Company moved from DUBLIN CAMP (A 10 d 6.8 Sheet 28) and relieved 150 M.G. Coy in line on YPRES-STADEN Railway - "A" Section in front line 2 guns North & 2 guns South of Railway in consolidated shell holes. "B" Section (8 guns) in barrage positions near OLGA HOUSES "C" Section (4 guns) in reserve on anti-aircraft work near Coy HQ. Company HQrs - U18 c 5.6 - (Sheet 20). Owing to dampness thick of cover had section was relieved every two days.	
	2nd		Enemy shelled 18 pdr Howitzer lines with gas shells during night. 2/3rd - Gas blew over Company HQ and helmets were worn though there was little concentration	
	3rd		The division on right attacked and S.O.S. signal was given - barrage guns fired 4 belts per gun + 500 rds. Their openen fire within 10 seconds of the signal being given. Front system fired one belt per gun to ensure that guns were all in working order. Intersection relief. 1 O.R. wounded.	

A.5834. Wt. W4973/M687. 750,000 8/16 D. D. & L. Ltd. Forms/C.2118/13.

Army Form C. 2118.

WAR DIARY
or
INTELLIGENCE SUMMARY.

(Erase heading not required.)

137 M.G. Coy.

Place	Date	Hour	Summary of Events and Information	Remarks and references to Appendices
U.18 c.5.6 (Sheet 20)			NOVEMBER 1917	
	4		Enemy aircraft active - bombs fell in Dublin Camp.	
	5		Intersection relief. 1 O.R. wounded	
	6		Practice bombardment started 6.45 am. Barrage of one belt in 5 minutes fired for 45 minutes. 1 O.R. wounded. 1 O.R. Killed. Throughout the tour enemy aeroplanes came over in early mornings & fired on groups of men & They did little damage and were driven off by M.G. fire. Two front guns other others North of Railway were superseded by 53rd Company - not taking over same positions.	
DUBLIN CAMP	7		Remaining guns relieved by 4 guns of 149 Company Company in DUBLIN CAMP. (A.10 & 6.9 Lt. Kellett - 2 O.R. wounded Sheet 28.	
	8		Company Reorganisation and preparation for moving.	
	9		8th - Coy strength - 9 officers 174 O.R.	

Army Form C. 2118.

WAR DIARY
or
INTELLIGENCE SUMMARY. 151st M.G.Coy

(Erase heading not required.)

Place	Date	Hour	Summary of Events and Information	Remarks and references to Appendices
MOULLE	NOVEMBER 1917			
	10.		Moved from DUBLIN CAMP. Company (Less Transport) travelled by train from ELVERDINGHE to WATTEN - then marched to billets near MOULLE - Company Headquarters Transport at farm - Q.6.a. 8.7. (Sheet 27A.S.E.) Sections billeted in neighbouring farms. Transport were two days journey to road, arriving on the afternoon of 11th.	
	11.		Two officers (2/Lieuts. Flanders & Maddocks) and 19 O.R. from x Division 50th Depot Battalion rejoined the Company. 13 O.R. reinforcements arrived.	
	12 to 14.		Reorganization & preparation for training.	
	15 to 30.		Training carried out according to Programme attached. Afternoons devoted to Recreational Training	

Army Form C. 2118.

WAR DIARY
or
INTELLIGENCE SUMMARY.

(Erase heading not required.)

151 M.G. Coy.

Instructions regarding War Diaries and Intelligence Summaries are contained in F. S. Regs., Part II. and the Staff Manual respectively. Title pages will be prepared in manuscript.

Place	Date	Hour	Summary of Events and Information	Remarks and references to Appendices
MOULLE			NOVEMBER 1917	
	14		One officer (2/LT M.T.J. KEENS) and 36 OR reinforcements arrived	
	15		Company Strength (10 officers 221 ORs.)	
	20		B. G. C. Inspected Transport	
	22		Company Strength 10 officers 220 ORs	
	24		Brigade Field Day	
	27		Brigade sports arranged but cancelled owing to weather conditions	
	29		Company Strength 10 officers 119 OR	

D. White, Capt.
O.C. 151 M.G. Coy

COPY.

Map Ref
Sheet :-
24a. S.W.

TRAINING PROGRAMME
151st MACHINE GUN COMPANY.

From: 15th November 1917, To: 24th November 1917 (incl.)

Date.	Time.	Outline of Training	Locality.	Remarks.
THURS: 1917 15th November	8.0 a.m. to 1.0 p.m.	Physical Training and Gun Drill	✱Coy. Parade Ground.	
FRI: 16th November	9 p.m. to 1.0 p.m.	Inspection followed by Route March	Inspection ✱Coy. Parade Ground	
SAT: 17th November	8.0 a.m. to 1.0 p.m.	Physical Training Squad Drill Gun Drill. also on German Gun.	✱Coy. Parade Ground.	
SUN: 18th November	—	Baths and Interior Economy.	Billets (Church)	(Sunday)
MON: 19th November	8.0 a.m. to 1.0 p.m.	Physical Training Miniature Range (using ?????)	Q.11.B.9.8.	
TUES: 20th November	8.0 a.m. to 1.0 p.m.	Lots of Elementary Training.	✱Coy. Parade Ground	
WED: 21st November	8.0 a.m. to 1.0 p.m.	Route March – London Drill.	P.24.C.N.D.	
THURS: 22nd November	8.0 a.m. to 1.0 p.m.	Observation of Ground. Writing Reports.	—	
FRI: 23rd November	—	Brigade Training.		
SAT: 24th November	8.0 a.m. to 1.0 p.m.	Laying Guns for Indirect Fire.		

A. daily class for Sergts. in Map Reading. ✱Coy: Parade Ground G.6.B.6.6. (Signed) D. Hamilton Capt.
151st M.G. Coy.

Ref. that
27. P. S W.

151st Machine Gun Coy.
Programme of Training
From 25th November 1917 to 30th November 1917 (incl.)

Date	Time	Outline of Training	Locality	Remarks
1917 25th November	8.30 a.m. To 12.30 p.m. 5.30 p.m. to 6 p.m.	Squad with Pack Saddle Drill Gun Drill	× Coy Parade	
26th November	8.30 a.m. to 1.0 p.m.	Sections in Attack and Defence	C Coy	
27th November	—	Interior Economy — Short	Billets	
28th November	8.30 a.m. to 1.0 p.m.	Sections practising laying Guns for Barrage Shoot	C Coy	
29th November	8.30 a.m. to 1.0 p.m.	Sub Sections on Range Sub Sections Knee Mount—& pack carry in & action from Line of Transport.	6.3.N – 6. 32.N.70	
30th November	8.30 a.m. to 1.0 p.m.	Company in Rearguard Action	× Coy Parade Ground Q.6.A.66.	

28/11/917

(Sgd) F. Nadder Capt
Comdg 151st M. G. Coy.

VOLUME XXIII   Confidential

War Diary

of

151ST Machine Gun Coy.

From Decr 1st 1917

To Decr 31st 1917

Army Form C. 2118.

WAR DIARY
or
INTELLIGENCE SUMMARY.
(Erase heading not required.)

151st 179 G. Co.

Place	Date	Hour	Summary of Events and Information	Remarks and references to Appendices
MOULLE	DECEMBER 1917			
	1.		Company at MOULLE.	
		16.8	Coy. HQ & Transport at Q 6 a 8.7 (Sheet 27.17) - Sections in neighbouring farms. Company training carried out as per attached training programme.	
	2.		Afternoon devoted to Recreations training (Sunday) Church Parade.	
	7.		C of E. Parade addressed by Bishop GWYNNE, G.C.F.	
	3.)		Company Strength - 10 Officers 179 OR.	
	8.		40 O.R. Langlaises to 243 Hd. Coy.	
			Divisional Sports	
			Moving orders received - Packing preparations for moving.	
	9.		Transport (less two limbers, water cart, chargers) moved by road to units Transport of 150 Infantry Brigade. Company attached to 150 Infantry Bde.	
BRANDHOEK	10.		Marched off 7.15am - proceeded by rail from WATTEN to BRANDHOEK arriving about 2 pm. Marched to RIDGE CAMP at G 11 a 4.3 (Sheet 28). Transport which had preceded by road arrived in camp 4.4g	

WAR DIARY or INTELLIGENCE SUMMARY

Army Form C. 2118.

151ST M.G. Coy

Place	Date	Hour	Summary of Events and Information	Remarks and references to Appendices
BRAND-HOEK	December 1917	about 3.30 p.m.	Remainder of Transport (two limbers), went out & Charabanc proceeded by rail from ST OMER to HOPOUTRE. Sections moved from camp at 5.15 am	
POTIJZE	11.		BRANDHOEK to YPRES - marched to POTIJZE - proceeded in April from Camp M.G. No 2. occupied by 248 M.G.Coy. Transport followed by road. Camp (M.G. 2) & I 3 d 1.4. (sheet 28) 151st M.G. Companies & 1st and 2nd Divisions (149th 150th 151st & 242nd) were amalgamated to form M.G. Groups under Lt Col. Harper D.M.G.O. 5th Div. held the line as follows:- 1 Coy (12 guns) in forward positions. 2 Companies in reserve camp at POTIJZE.	
IN THE LINE			Night 11/12th. Twelve guns relieved 12 guns of 248 M.G. Coy in Battery positions taking over tripods, S.A.A. &c as lunch stores. In going teams were subjected to a heavy quantity of shell gas - many men were seen coughing but the effects quickly passed off. Positions were taken up as follows:- "B" Section in switch line position & S.A.A. work site 2.	

Army Form C. 2118.

WAR DIARY
or
INTELLIGENCE SUMMARY.
(Erase heading not required.)

151 M.G. Coy

Place	Date	Hour	Summary of Events and Information	Remarks and references to Appendices
POTIJZE & IN THE LINE			DECEMBER 1917	
	12 to 15		"C" Section on S.O.S. lines & A.A. work. "D" Section on S.O.S. lines. Company advanced HdQrs at TYNE COTT. D.16.b.95.15. (Sheet 28) (inclusive) Company in the Line.	
	13.		Company strength 10 offrs 179 OR. 248 M.G. Coy moved out of Camp. 1 OR wdd in the line.	
	15.		3 OR wounded — (shell fire). night 15/16th Coy was relieved by 149th M.G. Coy and returned to camp at POTIJZE. Company in Camp at POTIJZE. (In Reserve)	
	16 to 19			
	17.		Reinforcements 1 OR (Sergeant) arrived.	
	20 to 23		night 19/20th Company relieved the 248th M.G. Coy in the line (forward positions). During the four days the line was moved with great boy strength 10 offrs 174 OR.	
	20.			
	21.		Reinforcements — 10 OR arrived	
	23.		1 OR wounded (M.G. fire). night 23/24th Coy was relieved by 149 M.G. Coy & returned to Camp	Nos. 3

Army Form C. 2118.

WAR DIARY
or
INTELLIGENCE SUMMARY.
(Erase heading not required.)

Instructions regarding War Diaries and Intelligence Summaries are contained in F. S. Regs., Part II. and the Staff Manual respectively. Title pages will be prepared in manuscript.

Place	Date	Hour	Summary of Events and Information	Remarks and references to Appendices
POTIJZE & IN THE LINE	24/6		at POTIJZE. Company in Reserve at POTIJZE.	
	27/5			
	27		Coy Strength 10 Officers 183 O.R. night 27/28 Company relieved 248 M.G.Coy in Barrage positions.	
	28/6/31		Company in Barrage positions in the line.	
	28		Reinforcements 10 O.R. arrived	
	29		Capt Ralston proceeded on leave to U.K. — Lt Armijones acting O.C.	

W.C.B. Jones
O.C. 1st M.G.Coy.

COPY.

2/11/1914

151st MACHINE GUN COMPANY.

PROGRAMME OF TRAINING
From 1st DECEMBER, 1914, TO 8th DECEMBER 1914. (both incl.)

DATE.	TIME.	Outline of Training.	Locality.	Remarks
1917. 1st DECEMBER ✗	8.30 p.m. to 1.0 p.m.	Section Competitions – Coming into action from limbers.	a. 22.o.+B (Shut 2yo.).	
3rd DEC.	8.30 a.m. to 1.0 p.m.	Physical training. Advanced Gun Drill &c.	"C" Area.	
4th DEC.	8.30 a.m. to 1.0 p.m.	Coy. Route March. Gun Drill.	—	
5th DEC.	8.30 a.m. to 1.0 p.m.	Physical training. Disposal of Section Officers.	C. Area.	
6th DEC.	8.30 a.m. to 1.0 p.m.	Laying Guns for Indirect Fire.	C. Area.	
7th DEC.	8.30 a.m. to 1.0 p.m.	Physical Training. Disposal of Section Officers.	Coy. Parade Ground.	
8th DEC.	8.30 a.m. to 1.0 p.m.	Range	a. 21.o. and a. 22.o.+B (Shl.2yp.)	

✗ Dec. 2nd – SUNDAY – SPORTS &c.

(Sd.) Jones Lt.
Comdg. 151st Machine Gun Company.

1/12/1914.

Army Form C. 2118.

WAR DIARY
or
INTELLIGENCE SUMMARY.
(Erase heading not required.)

WAR DIARY
OF THE
151st MACHINE GUN COMPANY
FROM 1st TO 31st JANUARY 1918.

VOLUME XXIV

L. Maples Capt.
O.in C. 151 M.G.Coy.

Army Form C. 2118.

151st Machine Gun Coy.

WAR DIARY
or
INTELLIGENCE SUMMARY.

(Erase heading not required.)

Place	Date	Hour	Summary of Events and Information	Remarks and references to Appendices
IN THE LINE AT POTIJZE.	1st		Sections were relieved from the line in the PASSCHENDAELE sector in the early morning and returned to Reserve Camp at POTIJZE.	
	2nd 3rd 4th		Days spent in making preparations for leaving the area. Company Strength 10 officers 191 O.R.	
			Transport moved by road starting at 8.30 a.m. for LECKE. Sections marched into YPRES and were conveyed from there by buses to WINNIZEELE. Marched towards LECKE. Intended billets were still occupied so the whole company spent the night in a farm at Q.9 & 9.7. (Sheet 27).	
LECKE.	5.		Company proceeded to billets nearer LECKE. Company H.Q. Transport and one Section in farm at Q.15 & 3.4 (Sheet 27). Remaining Sections were billeted in neighbouring farm.	
	6. 6. 15. 11.		Company training was carried out in accordance with training programme attached. Company Strength – 10 officers 175 O.R.	

WAR DIARY or INTELLIGENCE SUMMARY

Army Form C. 2118.

151 Machine Gun Coy

Place	Date	Hour	Summary of Events and Information	Remarks and references to Appendices
	January 1918			
FECKE	13		Capt. D. Ralston (O.C.) returned from Leave to U.K.	
	14		Transport Inspection by G.O.C. 50 Div.	
	16		Transport commenced a two days journey by road to the new area.	
	17		Company moved by rail. Entrained at CAESTRE, detrained at WIZERNES. Marched to LE VAL D'ACUIN arriving in billets about 9 pm.	
LE VAL D'ACUIN	18 to 26		Company training carried out in accordance with Training Programme attached.	
	18		Company Strength 10 officers 172 O.R.	
	25		Company Strength 10 officers 173 O.R.	
	25		Transport proceeded to join 149 Inf Bde Transport so as to start with them on 26th on two days journey by road to POTIJZE.	

Army Form C. 2118.

WAR DIARY
or
INTELLIGENCE SUMMARY.

151st Machine Gun Coy

(Erase heading not required.)

Place	Date	Hour	Summary of Events and Information	Remarks and references to Appendices
POTIJZE & IN THE LINE	January 1918.			
	27		Company moved by train. Entrained at WIZERNES – detrained at ST JEAN and marched from there to reserve camp at POTIJZE, arriving about 4 pm.	
	28		Before dawn 9 guns teams relieved guns teams of 19th M.G. Coy in front line positions of PASSCHENDAELE Sector.	
	28 to 31		Company in the Line.	

J Watson Capt
O.C. 151st M.G. Coy

A5834 Wt. W4973/M687 750,000 8/16 D. D. & L. Ltd. Forms/C.2118/13.

151st M.G. Coy.

151st MACHINE GUN COMPANY
PROGRAMME OF TRAINING.
FOR PERIOD - January 7th TO 12th 1918. - (both incl.)

DATE.	TIME.	OUTLINE OF TRAINING	REMARKS.
1918 MONDAY. JAN. 7th	8.45 a.m. to 1.0 p.m.	Physical Training. Squad Drill. Arms Drill. Gun Drill.	Afternoons will be allotted to Recreational Training
TUESDAY - 8th	-do-	Physical Training. Company Drill. Instruction on Lewis Gun.	Classes in Map Reading Compass Reading will be held daily for Officers for (1) Sergts. - under C.O. (2) Cpls. L/Cpls. & N.C.O.'s under the C.S.M.
WEDNESDAY. - 9th	9.0 a.m. to 1.0 a.m.	ROUTE - MARCH	
THURSDAY. - 10th	8.45 a.m. to 1.0 p.m.	BATHS	
FRIDAY. - 11th	-do-	Physical Training. Squad Drill. Gun Drill. Revolver Practice.	Range work will be included as and when Ranges are allotted.
SATURDAY. - 12th	-do-	Physical Training. Laying Guns for Indirect Fire.	

7/1/1918.

(sgd) Am Jones m. Pt.
for Capt. Comdg.
151st Machine Gun Coy.

151st MACHINE GUN COMPANY.

COPY

PROGRAMME OF TRAINING
for Period - January 13th to 19th 1918.

DATE	TIME	OUTLINE OF TRAINING	REMARKS.
1918. SUNDAY. JAN. 13th	—	Church Parades.	All men will be allowed to attend Recreational Services for such Troops classes for such Troops Company Parade. to be held for 1 hr each day for (1) Sergts under O.C. (2) Cpls, Rfls + No.1 under the C.S.M.
MONDAY. 14th	8.45 a.m. To 1.0 p.m.	Physical Training Squad Drill a/c Drill Company Drill.	
TUESDAY. 15th	— do —	Physical Training Revolver Practice Preparation for Transport Move.	
WEDNESDAY. 16th	9.0 a.m. To 1.0 p.m.	— Route March —	Range Work will be included as soon as Ranges in the new Area are allotted.
THURSDAY 17th	—	— Moving —	
FRIDAY 18th	9.30 a.m. T.O. - 1.0 p.m.	Re-organization. Laying Guns for Indirect fire.	
SATURDAY 19th	8.45 a.m. To 1.0 p.m.	Physical Training Inspection of Gas Helmets. Gas Drill. Lecture - "Economy".	

(Sgd) R.M. Jones, S.M. Natal
for Capt Comdt 151st Machine Gun Coy.

COPY.

PROGRAMME OF TRAINING.
FOR THE 151st MACHINE GUN COMPANY.
FOR PERIOD JAN. 20th TO 26th 1918.

DATE.	TIME.	OUTLINE OF TRAINING.	REMARKS.
SUNDAY. JAN. 20th	8.45 A.M. TO 1.0 P.M.	Church Parades. Inspections &c.	Afternoons will be devoted to Recreational Training.
MONDAY. - 21st.	do	Range Work	
TUESDAY. - 22nd	do	do	Specialist Training (Scouting, Writing Reports, Map Reading &c) will be carried out during the mornings.
WEDNESDAY. - 23rd	do	do	
THURSDAY. - 24th	do	Route March with Probable Scheme.	
FRIDAY. - 25th	do	Gun Drill. Pack Saddle Drill.	
SATURDAY. - 26th	do	Mechanism and Stoppages.	

18/1/18.

H. M. JONES. M.C. Lt.
for Capt. Comdg. 151st Machine Gun Coy.

Volume XXV   Confidential

War Diary
of
151st Machine Gun Coy

From Feby 1st 1918

To Feby 28th 1918.

Army Form C. 2118.

151st M. Gun Coy.

WAR DIARY
or
INTELLIGENCE SUMMARY.
(Erase heading not required.)

Place	Date	Hour	Summary of Events and Information	Remarks and references to Appendices
IN THE LINE POTIJZE.	FEBRUARY 1918			
	1.		Company relieved from the Line in the "PASSCHENDAELE" Sector by 149 M.G.Coy.) before dawn. In reserve at POTIJZE Camp.	
	1 to 4/a			
	4.		Company strength 10 officers 173 O.R. Night 4/5th relieved 245 M.G.Company in the line —	
	5 to 8		Company in the Line	
	8		1 O.R. wounded. Company relieved by 149 M.G.Coy in the afternoon. Company strength 10 officers 175 O.R.	
	9 to 12		Company in reserve at POTIJZE Camp.	
	12.		Company relieved 245 M.G.Company in the Line during the afternoon —	
	13 to 16		Company in the Line.	

Army Form C. 2118.

WAR DIARY
or
INTELLIGENCE SUMMARY.

151 M.G. Coy

(Erase heading not required.)

Place	Date	Hour	Summary of Events and Information	Remarks and references to Appendices
			FEBRUARY 1918	
POTIJZE	15.		Company Strength 10 offrs 175 OR	
	17.		Company relieved before dawn by 149 M.G Coy - returned to POTIJZE Camp.	
	17/18/19		In reserve at POTIJZE.	
	20		Company moved back from line. Entrained at YPRES. Detrained at WIZERNES - marched to LE VAL D'ACQUIN - arrived 9.30 p.m. Occupied same billets as formerly. Transport moved to rear Transport lines near BUSSY BOOM.	
LE VAL D'ACQUIN	21.		Transport moved by road with Transport of 149 Suffolks - three days journey - arrived at LE VAL D'ACQUIN at 1 p.m on 23 rd	
	21 to 24		Company preparing for training etc.	
	22.		Company strength 10 officers 174 OR.	
	26		Reinforcement- (1 Sergt, 1 Lcpl + 2 men) from Base Depot	

WAR DIARY
or
INTELLIGENCE SUMMARY. 151st M G Coy

Army Form C. 2118.

(Erase heading not required.)

Place	Date	Hour	Summary of Events and Information	Remarks and references to Appendices
Le Val D'Acquin	25 to 28		FEBRUARY. Company training carried out as per attached programme. Afternoon each day devoted to recreational training.	

H.F.H. Capt.
O in dg 151 M.G. Coy

151st. M.G.Co.

24/2/18

PROGRAMME OF TRAINING
FOR 151st. MACHINE GUN COMPANY.
FROM 25th FEBRUARY 1918 TO 28th FEBRUARY 1918 (Both incl.)

DATE.	7.30 a.m. to 8.0 a.m.	9.15 a.m. to 10.15 a.m.	10.30 a.m. to 12.45 p.m.	REMARKS:-
MONDAY 25th	PHYSICAL TRAINING	SQUAD DRILL, ARMS DRILL AND SALUTING.	CLASSES "A", "B" & "C".	Class "A" - First Week. (For New Men). General Description, Mechanism, Stripping, and Immediate Actions. Instructors - (Cpl. Kyrkham, Lcpl. Poole, Pte. McIntyre)
TUESDAY 26th				Class "B" - Barrage Drill (for Officers and N.C.O's) as laid down in S.S. 192. Instructors (2nd Graham, Sergt. Connell)
WEDNESDAY 27th				Class "C" - (Not old Gun No's) Most of Elementary Map Reading. Use of compass, Protractor & scales & field Instructors (2nd Lieut. Hyams)
THURSDAY 28th				

24/2/1918.

Hyams 2nd Lt. for Capt.
Cmdg. 151st. MACHINE GUN COMPANY.

50th Divisional Troops

BECAME "C" COMPNNY 50th MACHINE GUN BATTALION

151st MACHINE GUN COMPANY

MARCH 1918

Army Form C. 2118.

WAR DIARY
or
INTELLIGENCE SUMMARY.

(Erase heading not required.) 151st M.G. Coy.

Instructions regarding War Diaries and Intelligence Summaries are contained in F.S. Regs., Part II. and the Staff Manual respectively. Title pages will be prepared in manuscript.

Place	Date	Hour	Summary of Events and Information	Remarks and references to Appendices
Rejie surp - { 70000 AMIENS } { 60000 } 62 c 66 E			MARCH 1918	
LE VAL B'PAUIN	6/7		Coy in G.H.Q reserve — to be ready to move at 24 hours notice — Training was carried out in accordance with the attached programme	
	8		Recreational training in the afternoon. Inter-Company competitions in football & cross country running	
			Warning order to move received at 2am. Entraining station ARQUES — probable time of entrainment 12 noon. Operation order received at 6am. Company to entrain at 3pm. Coy marched off at 10am via LUMBRES, WISERNES & WESTOVE — Arrived at ARQUES station at 2.30pm. Train left at 6pm	
GLISY	9		Detrained at LONGUEAU (near AMIENS) at 2am. Marched to billets in GLISY	
	10		Warning order for move received	
HARBONNIERES	11		Company proceeded by march route to HARBONNIERES. In Army reserve — on 24 hours notice to move.	
	12/to/21		At Harbonnieres — training carried out as per programme — attached	

Army Form C. 2118.

WAR DIARY
or
INTELLIGENCE SUMMARY.
(Erase heading not required.)

Place	Date	Hour	Summary of Events and Information	Remarks and references to Appendices
	MARCH 1918			
	13		Parties from 151 Inf Bde (including Lafone) reconnoitred points in III Corps area.	
			— EPEHY. GOUZEAUCOURT. RONSOY	
	18		Capt Ralston proceeded to VICKERS Course at ST ROCH, G.H.Q.	
	19		Area of METZ & GOUZEAUCOURT reconnoitred by Section Officers.	
	20		Capt Ralston returned — course cancelled.	
	21		Warning order to be ready to move on 12 hours notice received 8.45 a.m. Warning order to be ready to move on 1 hours notice received 11 a.m. Company moved at 4:30 pm — marched to GOUZEAUCOURT and entrained. Detrained at BRIE about 10:30 pm — marched to BOUVINCOURT arriving about 2.30 am (22nd). Transport moved by road.	
	22		Transport arrived at 2.30 pm. A & D Sections proceeded to take up battle positions in line running from K.19.a to K.32.b (Sheet 62c). B & D Sections in the front line. A Section in support position about 1.30 to 2.5 (Sheet 62c). The 24th Divn withdrew through this line during the evening followed closely by the enemy. Some good targets were engaged by two guns of F Section	

WAR DIARY
or
INTELLIGENCE SUMMARY.
(Erase heading not required.)

Army Form C. 2118.

Place	Date	Hour	Summary of Events and Information	Remarks and references to Appendices
	23.		Situated at K.19.c.77 (Sheet 62c). Owing to the situation on the Divisional right, were ordered to withdraw. This movement commenced at 3am (23rd). During the remainder of the day (22nd) all Transport were kept in the village of BOUVINCOURT but moved out & took out of the village owing to shelling (the enemy aeroplanes having been very active) and about 10pm moved back to ST CREPIN as few orders received from 151 Inf Bde to whom the Company was attached. A.B. & D. Sections fought a rearguard action to the SOMME -altogether taking up 4 different positions. C Section moved from ST CREPIN along with Transport to LE MESNIL where they took up positions to cover the withdrawal of 151 Inf Bde from CATELET. Transport then proceeded across the bridge at OMIE. All Sections got good shooting during this withdrawal but unfortunately several guns were lost just before crossing the SOMME owing to a mule team in O.15.d (Sheet 62c) having	

WAR DIARY
or
INTELLIGENCE SUMMARY.
(Erase heading not required.)

Army Form C. 2118.

Place	Date	Hour	Summary of Events and Information	Remarks and references to Appendices
	24		to be crossed and then being the bridge, the teams having practically no ammunition over. C Section on withdrawal from LE MESNIL took up successive positions until the river SOMME was reached and the Infantry had passed over to the Western side when they eventually crossed and took up positions about O15a to cover the western exit from LE MESNIL. The remaining section went back to the Transport which had moved to BARLEUX. C Section was withdrawn about 8am. The Company then moved back to FOUCAUCOURT where it went into billets. Towards evening orders were received to man a line a few hundred yards East of ESTRÉES. Seven guns were ordered up for this purpose and were in position before dusk.	
	25		At 9am the seven guns in position (ESTRÉES) were ordered to move along with 151 by Bde to MARCHÉLPOT where they took up positions along the railway running through T16a, T22a, T21d, T27a (Sheet 62c). This position was held until	

Place	Date	Hour	Summary of Events and Information	Remarks and references to Appendices
	26		-duck when orders were given for the line to retire to position running from ABLAINCOURT to GENERMONT. The withdrawal being effected during the night it was possible to wither the fighting lines to within a few hundred yards of the enemy line. The Transport moved back to P.O.W. Camp, West of FOUCAUCOURT and remained there until about midnight when it moved back to LAMOTTE en SANTERRE. During the morning the infantry made a further withdrawal to a line running East of ROSIERES. This withdrawal being without sufficient warning and all guns being in a front line it was found impossible to get guns away and support the Infantry in their withdrawal. Guns remained and fired to the last. All guns were destroyed before abandoning the position, except two which were captured. The remaining personnel withdrew to the village of CAIX where the night was spent	

WAR DIARY or INTELLIGENCE SUMMARY

Army Form C. 2118.

Place	Date	Hour	Summary of Events and Information	Remarks and references to Appendices
	MARCH 1918			
	27		About 5pm the transport moved back to VILLERS BRETONNEUX. The C.O. rode back to Batt. H.Q. and transport lines to obtain more guns. During this time the situation having become critical on the 8th Divn line. Lt. A.H. Jones M.C., Lt. R.W. Youngs, 2nd/Lt. H.A.I. Greening along with the remaining gun numbers went into the line as infantry. Lt. Jones distinguished himself in a counter attack during which he was wounded and remained firing a German light gun with great effect. Lt. Keen was also wounded. Eventually Lt. Jones returned to the transport lines bringing with him the German gun and staff remained at duty. During the night Lt. Youngs brought out the remaining personnel to CAIX.	
	28		Lt. J.A. Lauder, Lt. L.R. Butler M.C., and Lt. McCrahan arrived at H.Q. with all available men from transport lines. With these and the remaining personnel at CAIX it was possible to form	

WAR DIARY or INTELLIGENCE SUMMARY

Army Form C. 2118.

Place	Date	Hour	Summary of Events and Information	Remarks and references to Appendices
	March 1918		Ten guns found. Light gun under Lt Lauder & Graham took up positions in E.16 b.d (Sheet 66E) – two guns being kept in reserve at E.15.a (66). During the afternoon the whole line started to withdraw. Lt Lauder & Graham along with the eight guns, withdrew to Transport lines to await orders. The reserve sub-section along with C.O. and Lt Butler withdrew to DOMART where four teams were put into shelter and efforts made to get into communication with Divisional H.Q. for orders. These were obtained – instructions being that the whole of 151 M.G. Bn would assemble at D.18 b.J.S. (Sheet 66E) in the morning. Transport moved to DOMART about 9am and at night proceeded to ROUVREL crossing the river near CASTEL. Lts Lauder & Graham with their parties joined the Transport at ROUVREL.	

WAR DIARY or INTELLIGENCE SUMMARY

Army Form C. 2118.

Place	Date	Hour	Summary of Events and Information	Remarks and references to Appendices
	MARCH 1918			
	29		The 157th Inf. Bde. assembled at D.18 d 7 3 (Sheet 66E). The Gunners were holding the Eastern edge of the wood & high ground in D.8 v 9 (Sh. 66E). Lt. Butler with two guns took up positions about D.7 c 6.6 (Sh.66E). Not long after these guns were in position the French retired from the high ground in D.8 & 9 to a position in line with the guns. These were shortly afterwards came into action shelled up the enemy and the crest running through D.8 v & d (Sh.66E) also a field gun was engaged at a range of 2000 yards and silenced. Towards evening the line was ordered to retire to a position along the DEMUIN - MOREUIL ROAD. Lt. Butler took up positions with three guns (one further had been calved in) C.11.c (Sh.66E). Transport in the morning moved from BOUVES to ROYES.	

WAR DIARY
or
INTELLIGENCE SUMMARY.

Army Form C. 2118.

Place	Date	Hour	Summary of Events and Information	Remarks and references to Appendices
	MARCH 1918			
	30.		Transport moved from BOVES to SAINS EN AMIENOIS. About 4 pm Enemy attacked from Sc. Infantry of 20th Divn. retired through gun position. The guns then opened fire on the advancing enemy at a range of 600 yards, the advance being held up. The Infantry of 20th Divn. later returned to original line along road in C.17 a + b (SK 66J) - no further attack being made that night.	
	31.		About 2 pm the enemy made a more determined attack during back our line; guns retiring after the Infantry to a position about C.10 b + d (SK66J). The three guns were then withdrawn to North side of River LUCE to guard bridge at C 3 d 3.4. Transport started on three days trek to ARQUES. The half of the Company with the Transport marched	

Army Form C. 2118.

WAR DIARY
or
INTELLIGENCE SUMMARY.
(Erase heading not required.)

Place	Date	Hour	Summary of Events and Information	Remarks and references to Appendices
	March 1918		to SAKEUK and spent the night at station awaiting entrainment.	

Instructions regarding War Diaries and Intelligence Summaries are contained in F. S. Regs., Part II. and the Staff Manual respectively. Title pages will be prepared in manuscript.

Army Form C. 2118.

APPENDIX I

WAR DIARY
or
INTELLIGENCE SUMMARY.
(Erase heading not required.)

Instructions regarding War Diaries and Intelligence Summaries are contained in F. S. Regs., Part II. and the Staff Manual respectively. Title pages will be prepared in manuscript.

Place	Date	Hour	Summary of Events and Information	Remarks and references to Appendices
			MARCH 1918	
			Casualties	
	22.		1 OR killed. 2 OR wounded.	
	23.		2 OR wounded	
	26.		2 OR missing	
	27.		Lt. A.M Jones M.C. wounded at duty. Lt. M.J. Keens wounded.	
			10 OR wounded	
	28.		1 OR killed, 3 OR wounded	
	29.		2 OR wounded	
	31.		3 OR wounded 6 OR missing	

151st M.G.(o) Copy
For old Gun Nos.

151st MACHINE GUN COMPANY

TRAINING PROGRAMME,
From 3/3/1918 to 7/3/1918 (11th incl.).

DATE.	TIME.	LOCALITY.	NATURE OF TRAINING.
1918. 3rd	SUNDAY.		CHURCH PARADES & INSPECTIONS. ETC.
4th	7.30am to 8am	Coy. Parade Ground	Physical Training.
	9.0am to 10am	— do —	Squad and Arms Drill.
	10.0am to 12.30pm	— do —	Barrage Drill.
5th	7.30am to 8.0am		Physical Training.
	9.0am to 12.30pm	RANGE.	Stoppages and Instant rectifying work (knuckles rub by) the indirect and aiming posts.
6th	7.30am to 8.0am	Coy. Parade Ground	Physical Training.
	9.0am to 10.30am	— do —	Burning Pounder (triangle of error).
	10.30am to 12.30pm	— do —	Barrage Drill.
7th	7.30am to 8.0am	Coy. Parade Ground	Physical Training.
	9.0pm to 12.30pm	RANGE.	Stoppages and Instant rectifying work. Knuckles rub by the indirect and aiming posts.

2/3/1918.

(Sd) H. Ralston. Capt.
Comdg. 151st Machine Gun Company.

151st MACHINE GUN COMPANY.

TRAINING PROGRAMME

From 3/3/1918 to 7/3/1918 (4th incl.).

For "NEW" Gun No's:—

DATE	TIME	LOCALITY	NATURE OF TRAINING
1918 3rd (SUNDAY)	—	—	CHURCH PARADES, INSPECTIONS ETC.
4th	7.30 a.m. to 8.0 a.m.	Coy. Parade Ground	Physical Training
	9.0 a.m. to 12.30 p.m.	In Billets.	Belt Filling and Mechanism.
5th	7.30 a.m. to 8.0 a.m.	Coy. Parade Ground	Physical Training
	9.0 a.m. to 10.0 a.m.	Billets	Belt Filling
	10.0 a.m. to 11.0 a.m.	Coy. Parade Ground	Elementary Gun Drill
	11.0 a.m. to 12.30 p.m.	Billets	Mechanism
6th	7.30 a.m. to 8.0 a.m.	Coy. Parade Ground	Physical Training
	9.0 a.m. to 10.0 a.m.	Billets	Belt Filling
	10.0 a.m. to 11.0 a.m.	"	Rust and Polishing of Guns
	11.0 a.m. to 12.30 p.m.	"	Mechanism and Courtmail Action
7th	7.30 a.m. to 8.0 a.m.	Coy. Parade Ground	Physical Training
	9.0 a.m. to 11.0 a.m.	— At —	Contents of Gun Limbers and loading of Pack Saddles
	11.0 a.m. to 12.30 a.m.	Billets	Immediate Action

(Sgd). L. Ralston Capt.

Cmdg. 151st Machine Gun Company.

2/3/1918.

15th (Coy.) / M.G.C. / Gun Nos. :—

(&) O.K.D. Nos.:—   COPY.

151st MACHINE GUN COMPANY

TRAINING PROGRAMME from 14/3/1918 to 21/3/1918 (Half incl.)

DATE	TIME	LOCALITY	NATURE OF TRAINING
1918. 14th	8.30 a.m. to 12.30 p.m.	Coy. Parade Ground	ROUTE MARCH
15th	7.30 am to 8.0 am 9.0 am to 10.0 am 10.0 am to 11.30 am 11.30 am to 12.30 pm	— do — — do — — do — — do —	Physical Training Bayonet Drill Sympathetic Action between the Company Chronicles (?) Physical Training Gun Drill
16th	7.30 am to 8.0 am 9.0 am to 10.0 am 10.0 am to 11.0 am 11.0 am to 12.30 pm	Coy. Parade Ground — do — — do — — do —	Burial Parade — Funeral of Lieut. Squad & Arms Drill
17th	SUNDAY.		CHURCH PARADES. INSPECTIONS. ETC.
18th	7.30 am to 8.0 am 9.0 am to 10.0 am 10.0 am to 12.30 pm	Coy. Parade Ground — do — — do —	Physical Training Squad Drill and Arms Drill Bayonet Drill
19th	7.30 am to 8.0 am 9.0 am to 10.0 am 10.0 am to 12.30 pm	Coy. Parade Ground — do — — do —	Physical Training Squad Drill and Arms Drill Bayonet Work on Short Range
20th	8.30 am to 12.30 pm		ROUTE MARCH
21st	7.30 am to 8.30 am 9.0 am to 10.30 am 10.30 am to 12.30 pm	Coy. Parade Ground — do —	Physical Training Aiming Practice — Firing 15 rds of Blank Immediate Action on Short Range

*Coy. Parade Ground — Right at End of the Rue de Montcourt.

12/3/1918

(Sgd) R. Raleigh Capt.
Comdg. 151st Machine Gun Company

15¹ᵗ Coy.
M.G.C.

For new Gun Nos.

12/3/18

151ˢᵗ Machine Gun Company.

Copy.

TRAINING PROGRAMME from 14/3/1918 to 21/3/1918 (both incl.)

DATE.	TIME.	LOCALITY.	NATURE OF TRAINING.
1918. 14ᵗʰ	8.30 a.m. to 12.30 p.m.	?	ROUTE MARCH. —
15ᵗʰ	7.30am to 8.0am 9.0am to 10.0am 10.0am to 11.0am 11.0am to 12.30pm	Coy. Parade Ground — do — — do — — do —	Physical Training Gun Drill Belt filling Instruction on Structural test
16ᵗʰ	7.30am to 8.0am 9.0am to 10.0am 10.0am to 11.0am 11.0am to 12.30pm	Coy. Parade Ground — do — — do — — do —	Physical Training Gun Drill Immediate Action Mechanism
17ᵗʰ	SUNDAY.	—	CHURCH PARADES. + INSPECTIONS, ETC. —
18ᵗʰ	7.30am to 8.0am 9.0am to 12.30pm	Coy. Parade Ground — do —	Physical Training Mechanism Gun Drill &c.
19ᵗʰ	7.30am to 8.0am 9.0am to 10.0am 10.0am to 11.0am 11.0am to 12.30pm	Coy. Parade Ground — do — — do — — do —	Physical Training Belt filling Immediate Gun Drill Immediate action
20ᵗʰ	7.30am to 8.0am 9.0am to 11.0am 11.0am to 12.30pm	Coy. Parade Ground — do — — do —	Physical Training Instruction on the procedure adopted on Direct and Barrage Positions Immediate Relief and Mechanism
21ˢᵗ	7.30am to 8.0am 9.0am to 11.0am 11.0am to 12.30pm	Coy. Parade Ground — do — — do —	Physical Training Contents of Gun Limbers and the Loading of Pack saddles Immediate Action

*Coy. Parade Ground. — { Right of and at the Rue de Morecourt Ensée the — Rue de Morecourt

(Sgd) L. Ruston Capt.
Coy. 151ˢᵗ Machine Gun Company.

12/3/1918

www.ingramcontent.com/pod-product-compliance
Lightning Source LLC
Chambersburg PA
CBHW081408160426
43193CB00013B/2135